KARATE
everyone

Mike Sawyer

University of Florida

Clancy Moore, *Consulting Editor*

Hunter Textbooks Inc.
823 Reynolda Road
Winston-Salem, North Carolina 27104

To my loving wife Kim, who has stood by me always.

Cover by Deborah Dale Moore

Photograph on page 36 courtesy of Treco Products

Copyright 1985 by Hunter Textbooks Inc.

ISBN 0-88725-036-X

All rights reserved. No part of this publication may be reproduced in any form whatsoever without written permission of the publisher.

Inquiries regarding this book or others in this series should be addressed to:

PREFACE

Until recent years, karate was viewed by the public as a mystical art — as a secret capability that, once obtained, enabled a person to survive any attack. Black belts were seen as symbols of invincibility. How they, and the skills they represented, really developed, no one really knew. Popular myth had these martial artists gaining their skills through mystical experiences, secret ceremonies, and covert tests against vicious attackers and real weapons.

With the emergence of the martial arts "from the closet," so to speak, in the 1950s, karate began to be judged in a different light. The public's view of karate as a mystical art that just "imparted" knowledge and skills to practitioners was replaced by the more realistic visions of rooms full of trainees punching and kicking in unison to the instructor's count; of sweat-soaked uniforms and bodies being pushed to previously unknown physical limits; of meditation as a tool for physical and mental relaxation rather than as a pathway to "enlightenment," of martial knowledge and skill obtained through years of dedication and experience; and of children and adults learning about themselves — their limits of self-discipline, dedication, motivation, and confidence — and how far those limits could be developed.

Today, karate is seen for what it really is; a multifaceted art that combines elements of awareness, reflexes, and physical skill with confidence and belief in oneself. It is not a religion, but rather a unique addition to one's lifestyle. It is not mystical, but rather rational and pragmatic. It is not always what one might expect, but often much more: a way to achieve and maintain extraordinary conditioning while learning self-defense skills that can last a lifetime — or help prolong it!

A true study of the martial arts means not only learning techniques, but understanding the principles and philosophies behind each movement. *Karate Everyone* is designed as a complete training guide for the beginning and intermediate martial arts student. In addition to describing techniques, self-defense and free-fighting strategies, information covering flexibility, strength-building, and nutrition are included. The history of karate as an art and sport is also summarized, since it is essential for the student to know not only where karate is going, but also where it has been. The techniques selected for this book are the ones most suited for the beginner, and will provide the martial arts novice with both a practical working knowledge of self-defense, and a strong base from which to advance to the more sophisticated techniques and concepts of karate.

You will find that the word "karate," as used within the text, is a general term to define the empty-handed fighting arts, regardless of the country of origin. Although in truth an Okinawan or Japanese word, its common meaning in America has come to include all striking arts, including those from Okinawa, Japan, Korea, China and Burma. Instructors will find this book is designed for use by students of all styles, and is compatible with the style specifics as taught in the classroom.

Good luck in your quest for knowledge and skill in the art and sport of karate.

Acknowledgements

The author is indebted to many persons for helping to make this book possible.

Special thanks are in order to my parents, who encouraged early in my life an interest in literature; Sensei Newton Harris, who has been not only my karate instructor, but a supportive friend as well; and Dr. Clancy Moore, who believed in my writing abilities as well as my teaching.

Grateful acknowledgements should also be given to Michael McCoy, whose insight, support, and technical abilities contributed greatly to the text and pictures; and to my senior black belts, Chuck McCaughey, Pam Petrone, Doug Pierce, Hampton McRae, Joe Prentice, Kim Sawyer, Cory Schafer, and Chauka Fleming, who posed for pictures as well as providing suggestions and inspiration.

Credit should also go to Greg Young, who contributed much time posing for photos, and to Andree McRae, Laura Champbell, and Christie Jurney, who spent many hours typing the manuscript.

CONTENTS

Chapter		Page
1	Karate — Yesterday and Today	1
2	Questions Most Often Asked	11
3	Equipment and Facilities	29
4	The Mental Aspect	41
5	Conditioning for Karate	45
6	Developing Flexibility	61
7	Stances	71
8	Principles of Effective Technique	75
9	Hand Strikes	89
10	Kicks	109
11	Blocks	123
12	Use of Elbows and Knees	133
13	Breakfalls and Sweeps	141
14	Body Movement	151
15	Combinations (Putting Your Attack Together)	163
16	Getting Your Defense Together	177
17	Forms — Practicing for Perfection	185
18	Karate for Self-Defense	205
19	Karate for Sport	227
	Appendixes	247

Chapter 1
Karate — Yesterday and Today

WHY KARATE?

The tremendous surge of popularity that karate has enjoyed can be attributed to the curiosity of Americans and their love of anything sport-affiliated. Robert Trias held the first karate tournament in America in 1946, a mere nine years after bringing the art to the United States. By the mid-1950's, karate schools were popping up all over the country, as veterans of the Second World War and the Korean War began passing on the art they had embraced.

As exposure of the martial arts has grown nationally, helped by movies and the advent of the spectator-oriented full-contact version of the sport, Americans have taken to karate in a manner unprecedented by other combative art/sports. Hundreds of light-contact tournaments are held each year with men, women, and children of all walks of life as participants. Professional full-contact karate has a country-wide promotion circuit as well as a place on weekly national television.

As many as ten million Americans are taking karate lessons, according to recent estimates. This indicates that the vast majority are involved in karate for reasons other than the sporting aspects. Many see karate as the ultimate in a combined fitness/self-defense program, and appreciate the time efficiency such a dual program can offer. Many men and women seeking conditioning and/or weight control become bored with diets or "do-it-over-and-over" exercise routines and turn to karate as an alternative. Parents appreciate the discipline and winning attitude karate instills in children. Assault-conscious men and women find in karate a method of self-defense that relies on skill rather than strength or weapons. Many athletes turn to karate as a sport for the individual — a sport that relies on self-motivation rather than teamwork. However, most people take karate lessons to stay in shape, learn self-defense, and have fun.

The many benefits and facets of karate can make it the activity for you. Little equipment is needed and it can be practiced anywhere, including your own home. Karate knows no age limit, nor are there any limits of skill or knowledge. It can be a healthful activity that you will want to practice for many years to come.

HISTORY OF THE ART

Origins

It is almost universally accepted that the martial arts as we know them today began when the Indian monk Bodidharma traveled to China in the seventh century A.D. His purpose for the journey was to instruct Chinese monks in the ways of the Zen Buddhist religion. He settled at the Shaolin Temple in Honan Province, and found the monks there to be in very poor physical condition due to lack of exercise. He devised a system of exercises designed both to increase their level of fitness and to bring them some measure of defense against the thieves and robbers who preyed on them outside the confines of the temple.

Shaolin kung-fu, as this form of self-defense came to be known, eventually spread throughout the Chinese mainland and filtered into surrounding Oriental countries. Other countries, as we shall see in the following sections, built upon this knowledge to develop their own particular brands of martial arts.

China

During the seventh through sixteenth centuries A.D., Shaolin kung-fu continued to be refined and practiced at the Shaolin Temple at Honan. Seldom were the arts taught to persons other than the residing monks.

In the seventeenth century, anti-government revolutionaries took refuge in the temple, leading to its destruction by government forces. According to Chinese legend, only five monks escaped the destruction, and these five became the originators of the five forerunner styles of modern kung-fu: Hung, Tau, Mok, Choy, and Li.

The years since 1700 have seen the various styles of Chinese kung-fu increase both in number and popularity. Millions of Chinese practice the arts in their homeland, though large schools such as those found in the United States are virtually unknown in China due to economic conditions there. Most kung-fu in China is taught in residences or in small back-street schools.

Okinawa

The martial arts were first brought to the Okinawan Islands during the seventh century, probably by shipwrecked Chinese monks traveling to Japan. These contacts continued at infrequent intervals

Yesterday and Today 3

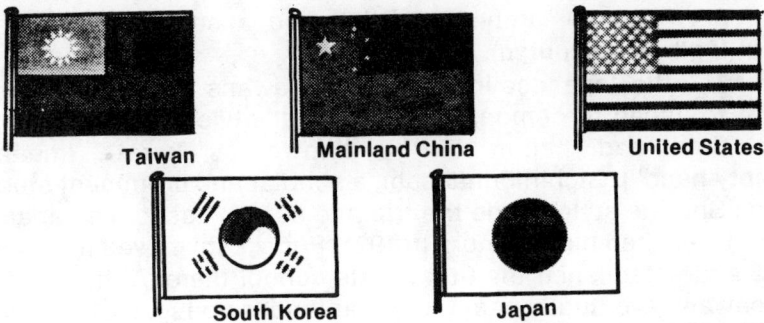

for the next seven hundred years, and a primitive form of Okinawan karate developed from the islanders' practice of the Chinese kung-fu arts. In the fourteenth century, official Chinese-Okinawan trade and diplomatic channels were opened, and the Chinese who traveled to Okinawa began openly teaching kung-fu to the Okinawans.

The Okinawan government banned all weapons on the Island in 1429, and weaponless forms of combat grew even faster in popularity. In 1609 Japanese invaders conquered the Okinawans and again imposed a weapons ban. The Okinawans, forced to defend themselves against their country's captors with only their bare hands and feet, began to unify under the well-known karate masters and organize their fighting systems into what would eventually become the various Okinawan styles.

By the eighteenth century, three main styles of karate emerged in Okinawa, as taught by the three most prominent masters. The names of the styles were taken after the cities in which they became popular — the coastal cities of Naha and Tomari and the capital city of Shuri. These three styles, *Naha-te* (under Master Kanryo Higashionna), *Tomari-te* (under Master Hosaku Matsumora), and *Shuri-te* (under Master Karate Sakugawa), became the foundation for all modern styles of Okinawan and Japanese karate.

Since the early 1900s, karate has remained nearly unchanged in Okinawa. This may be due in great part to the geographical remoteness of the island. The major styles presently are *Goju-ryu* (probably the most popular), *Uechi-ryu,* and *Shorin-ryu. Isshin-ryu* and *Kempo* are practiced to a more limited extent.

Japan

Although often thought of as the world's stronghold of karate, Japan actually had a late start in its martial arts development. Until the 1920's, knowledge of the empty-handed striking arts were limited to some military units who had traveled to China and Okinawa, and a few widely-scattered Buddhist temples founded by traveling Chinese monks. Japan's rich feudal history of samurai warriors and military endeavors led martial arts interest among the people to center more around the traditional Japanese arts of swordplay (kendo), archery (kyudo), and a self-defense type of wrestling/boxing (jujitsu).

In 1917, the Japanese invited the Okinawans to send a representative to Japan to demonstrate Okinawan-style fighting, which by that time had begun to be known as **karate** (meaning "empty-hand"). Gichin Funakoshi, a scholar and prominent student of the Shuri-te style, made the trip and so impressed the Japanese that they invited him to return in 1921. Funakoshi moved to Japan in 1922 and established the first karate school there. Although other Okinawans eventually came to Japan and introduced other styles, Funakoshi is generally credited with first popularizing the art, and thus is commonly called the "Father of Modern-Day Karate." The style Funakoshi developed, the *Shotokan* style (after Funakoshi's pen name of "Shoto"), still has the largest following worldwide of any of the Japanese styles.

The Japanese people took to karate with a passion almost immediately. Membership in the various schools climbed steadily, and new styles appeared as many Okinawan masters immigrated to Japan to spread their arts. Today they are four major systems in Japan: Shotokan, Wado-ryu (founded by the late Hironori Otsuka in the 1920s), *Shito-ryu* (brought to Japan from Okinawa by Kenwa Mabuni in the 1920s), and *Goju-ryu* (organized under Gogen Yamaguchi, who arrived from Okinawa in the 1920s). Other prominent styles include *Kyokushinkai* (under the legendary Mas Oyama), *Koei-kan* (under Eizo Onishi), *Chito-ryu* (under Tsuyoshi Chitose), and *Rembukai* (under M. Koide).

Korea

During the ninth and tenth centuries, descendants of the original followers of Bodidharma traveled to Korea on religious missions. The knowledge of the Chinese fighting arts they brought with them was combined with the primitive forms of empty-handed combat already being practiced on the Korean peninsula. The result, termed *Soo Bak,* spread openly throughout Korea during the next five hundred years.

During the years 1400-1850, the martial arts fell into steep decline in Korea, and it was not until the Sino-Japanese War of 1894 that Soo Bak appeared publicly. The name was changed at that time to *Tang Soo Do,* which means "art of the Chinese hand" in Korean. The arts took on a distinct military slant during the subsequent period of Japanese occupation. When Korea was liberated from the Japanese in 1945, Tang Soo Do again flourished, and in 1955 the name was changed to Tae Kwon Do, which means the "way of striking with the hands and feet." Today, Tae Kwon Do reigns as one of Korea's major national sports, and training in the art is required in both the public schools and the military. Although known generically as Tae Kwon Do, the Korean arts have developed into several distinct major styles, including *Moo Duk Kwan, Ji Do Kwan,* and *Chung Do Kwan.*

United States

The martial arts arrived in the United States during the last half of the nineteenth century, when Chinese immigrants were brought to the West Coast as railroad workers. Although Americans were aware of the strange fighting styles of the Chinese, the Orientals kept their knowledge of kung-fu strictly among their own communities. Knowledge was passed mainly from parents to children, and during the first part of the twentieth century many kung-fu clubs could be found in the Chinatowns of San Francisco, Los Angeles, and New York. Non-Chinese were not accepted as students until the early 1960s, over a hundred years after kung-fu first entered this country.

Karate was brought to Hawaii in the early 1930s by Okinawan visitors and immigrants, and the first karate club composed of Caucasians was organized in 1933.

Karate finally reached the mainland in 1946, when Robert Trias, who had studied Shorei-ryu karate while stationed in Okinawa during World War II, began teaching in Phoenix, Arizona. In 1952, Japan's colorful Mas Oyama, a legendary fighter and founder of the Kyokushinkai ("Ultimate Truth") style of karate, toured the United States giving spectacular demonstrations, including the defeat of a professional boxer in New York's Madison Square Garden. His visit and the accompanying publicity helped spark an interest among Americans in karate.

In 1955 Tsutomu Ohshima, a top student of Gichin Funakoshi, began teaching the Shotokan style in Los Angeles. In 1958 Jhoon Rhee, who would later attain great fame and fortune as the instructor of many top karate champions and the inventor of the first protective hand-and-foot karate equipment, began teaching Korean Tae Kwon Do karate in Texas. The martial arts were off and running in America.

By the late 1950s schools of mostly Okinawan and Japanese were established throughout the continental United States, mostly by Far East immigrants and returning servicemen. The early 1960s saw a large immigration of Korean Tae Kwon Do instructors, a trend that would continue into the 1970s.

Four superstars of tournament karate emerged in the 1960s — Joe Lewis, Chuck Norris, Mike Stone, and Skipper Mullins — and karate as a sport became firmly entrenched. Among them, these men won nearly every major tournament in existence and set the standards for excellence in tournament karate competition.

In the mid-1960s Joe Corley, a Tae Kwon Do student in Atlanta, broke from the Korean system and established himself as a teacher of "American Karate." It was a bold move, but it encouraged others who had become dissatisfied with strictly-controlled Oriental systems. Soon there were numerous "American style" schools in the Southeastern United States. Corley later became one of America's leading authorities on the full-contact version of sport karate, and now acts as expert commentator for many television broadcasts of the sport.

The second-generation of American karate practitioners — those trained in the United States by the original pioneers — began to strike out on their own and open schools in the 1960s and early 1970s. These included such notables as Frank Ruiz (Nisei Goju-Ryu), John Worley (Tae Kwon Do), Allen Steen (Tae Kwon Do), and Jay T. Will (Kempo).

The American media began to take notice of karate in the mid-1970s. The movie *Billy Jack* in 1972 and a sequel two years later brought the martial arts onto the silver screen, and a trio of movies by Bruce Lee — *Fists of Fury* (1972), *(Way of the Dragon* (1972) and *Enter the Dragon* (1973) — drew large audiences nationwide. The weekly television series, *Kung-Fu,* began in 1972, and the words "karate" and "kung-fu" quickly became household words.

The face of sport karate was changed for all time in 1974: the first World Championships were fought with safety pads and full contact in Los Angeles. This event gave birth to a sport now seen weekly on television by millions. After those championships, the best of the karate tournament fighters began to try full-contact competition, and World Middleweight Champion Bill "Superfoot" Wallace became full-contact karate's first superstar. Wallace was known for his lightning-fast kicks, and his skills attracted the attention of the major television networks. Many of his title defenses between 1974 and his retirement in 1980 were televised nationally, and karate as a spectator sport received a tremendous boost. Wallace became the most famous karate competitor of all time and continues to teach and appear occasionally in exhibition matches.

Tournament light-contact karate took a backseat to full-contact events for a few years, but in 1978 a new star emerged. Keith Vitali, an athletic black belt and ex-runner from the University of South Carolina, moved to Atlanta and began to travel to — and win — most of the major United States tournaments. His flashy style and confidence made him a favorite of the fans, and his superior technique and crafty fighting style carried him to the top spot among America's black belt competitors in 1978, 1979 and 1980. He retired early in 1981 at the age of 28, but left behind a revitalized tournament karate circuit.

KARATE TODAY

In America, karate has become an art and sport practiced and/or watched by millions, and has gained much more publicity than the early Oriental instructors could have imagined possible. Every major city contains schools of various styles, and even smaller towns nearly always have some location where karate is taught. Most schools designed for the public concentrate on fitness and self-defense, and some contain modern fitness equipment such as weight machines, saunas, whirlpool baths, and steamrooms. Huge schools with extensive facilities and multiple workout floors are becoming commonplace in the larger cities, although one can still find the small, plain karate school typical of karate's formative years. Training for both light- and full-contact competition is usually available at selected schools, but is nearly always secondary to the function as a training center for self-defense.

Styles have changed greatly from past years and, while basic styles are still taught traditionally at some schools, most schools offer a version of a traditional style that has undergone some degree of "modernization." The classical forms and traditions exist in a format that also includes the latest advances in self-defense skills, strategies, and fitness training. Most schools make extensive use of protective equipment during sparring practice and modern equipment aids, such as striking bags and stretching machines, have gained widespread favor.

Although nearly all styles of karate have enjoyed widespread exposure across the country, some trends still can be seen. Chinese kung-fu styles are in greater abundance in the Western and Northeastern United States than in other areas, while the Midwest and adjoining areas contain many Okinawan-style schools. Japanese styles enjoy large followings in California and the East Coast, while Korean styles are fairly evenly distributed across the country.

Yesterday and Today

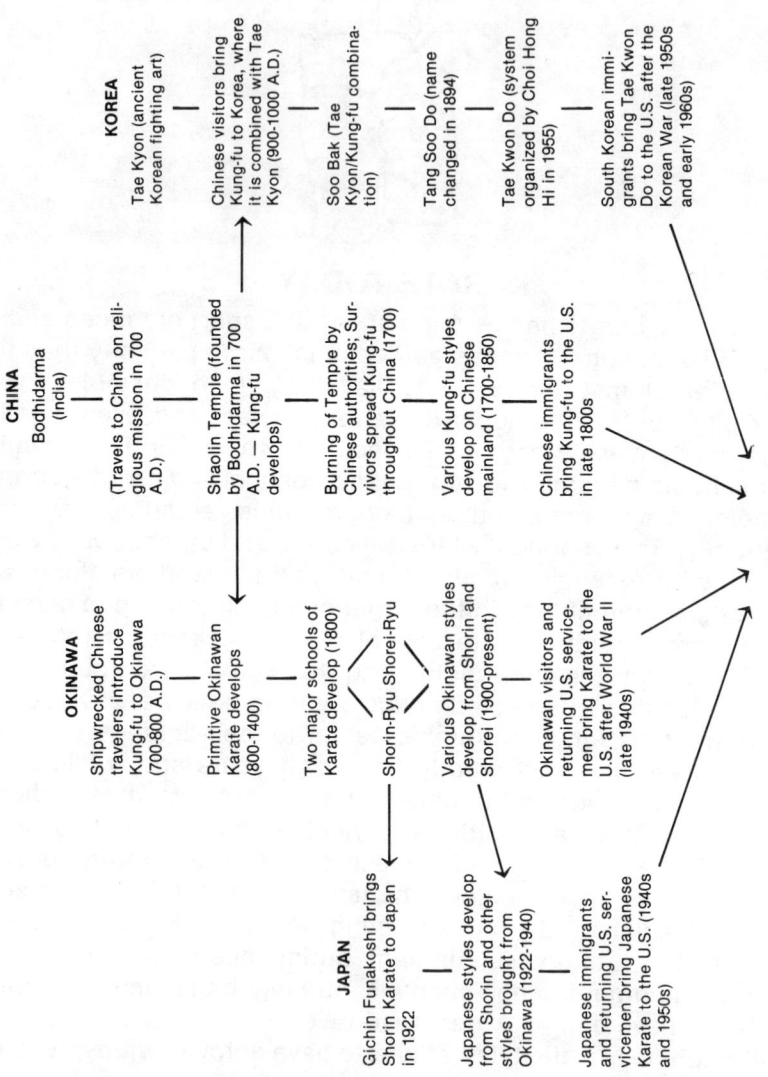

CHAPTER 1 EVALUATION

Multiple Choice: Circle the letter of the correct answer.

1. The number of Americans currently in karate programs across the country has been estimated to be as high as:
   a. one million
   b. five million
   c. ten million
   d. 15 million

2. Shaolin Kung-fu was first brought to Okinawa during the:
   a. sixth century
   b. seventh century
   c. eighth century
   d. ninth century

3. The name Korean karate is known generically as is:
   a. Tae Kwon Do
   b. Tang Soo Do
   c. Chung Do Kwan
   d. Hwa Rang Do

4. The man who brought karate to Japan in 1917 and who became known as the "Father of Modern-Day Karate" was:
   a. Bodidharma
   b. Karate Sakugawa
   c. Robert Trias
   d. Gichin Funakoshi

5. The four major styles of Japanese karate include all of the following except:
   a. Shotokan
   b. Shito-ryu
   c. Wado-ryu
   d. Shorin-ryu

Fill in the blanks:

1. The Indian monk _____ traveled to China in the _____ century A.D., bringing with him knowledge of the martial arts.

2. The forerunner of modern Tae Kwon Do was practiced widely on the Korean peninsula during the _____ through the _____ centuries, and was known as _____.

3. The three main Okinawan systems of karate during the seventeenth and eighteenth centuries were named after the cities in which they became popular, and were known as _____-te, _____-te, and _____-te.

4. Modern-day karate styles can be traced to four primary countries of origin, including _____, _____, _____, and _____.

5. The United States first received martial arts exposure in the latter half of the _____ century, from immigrants from the country of _____.

6. Karate as we know it today reached the U.S. mainland in _____ when _____ returned from duty overseas and began teaching _____ryu in Phoenix, Arizona.

7. The legendary karate fighter _____, who also founded the **Kyokushinkai** style of karate, visited the U.S. in _____ and helped publicize karate across America.

8. The inventor of the first prototype of the safety equipment karate students use today, Master _____, began teaching _____ type karate in _____ in 1958.

9. The first World Middleweight Full-Contact Karate Champion, who became the most famous karate competitor in history, was _____.

Chapter 2
QUESTIONS MOST OFTEN ASKED

CAN ANYONE, AT ANY TIME, BECOME INVOLVED IN KARATE?

Yes. Karate is beneficial at nearly any age and is equally suitable for men and women. Even young children who perceive differently the sport and self-defense aspects still benefit greatly from the coordination, concentration, fitness, and discipline. Juniors and young adults may be interested in the sport potential, while older persons may benefit more from the exercises, self-defense training, and mental stress reduction.

Handicapped persons needn't feel that they cannot progress just as well as the nonhandicapped. Their training program may be adjusted to accommodate their particular handicap. The versatility of karate makes it one of the most suitable physical activities for the handicapped.

BUT DON'T I NEED TO GET INTO SOME KIND OF SHAPE BEFORE I START CLASS?

This is one of the most common questions a karate instructor hears, and the answer is an emphatic "No!". Beginning karate classes are designed not only for those without previous karate knowledge, but also for those whose physical training has been limited. Beginning programs are tailored for the complete novice, not the athlete who intends to learn a new skill. (Many athletes do become involved in karate programs, however, to improve their performance in their primary sport. These students generally progress faster and quite often enter the intermediate level ahead of schedule.) Don't worry about conditioning yourself before joining a class. You'll only delay your progress. Get involved, and let your instructor tell you what kind of conditioning program you should follow concurrent to your karate class schedule.

WILL MY KARATE WORKOUTS HELP ME LOSE WEIGHT?

Any physical exercise forces your body to burn calories at an accelerated rate. The more taxing the exercise, the more calories you burn. It is likely that the karate techniques will be interesting and motivating so that you will look forward to practice sessions. This frequent, concentrated exercise will increase your circulation and heart rate, and greatly increase your body's consumption of stored calories. This will result in a safe, progressive, reduction of body fat that will be permanent — provided that you don't eat all those calories back on. Weight loss through exercise is certainly the preferred way, and the fast-slow movements of karate are ideal. However, any weight loss will only be lasting if combined with safe, common sense eating habits.

Additionally, the strengthening exercises you participate in as part of your karate conditioning program help you slim up in two ways: one, they burn even more of your stored calories; and two, they help firm up crucial areas, such as the abdomen, hips, buttocks and thighs, that become flabby through fat storage and muscular disuse.

WILL MY WORKOUTS INCREASE STAMINA ALSO?

Yes. During the exercise portion of your classes (and in your own practice time outside of class), you will notice your breathing and heart rate increase, and initially you may feel quite out of breath at times. Your body's reaction to this will be to upgrade your entire respiratory and circulatory system to handle the new workload. Your heart (really a muscle) will become stronger, new blood vessels will open to carry and increase blood supply, and your body's overall ability to process oxygen will be increased.

HOW LONG WILL IT TAKE ME TO BECOME PROFICIENT AT KARATE?

As a beginner, you will learn a large amount of material quickly. In each class you will learn something you didn't know before, and practicing outside of class will help make what you have learned permanent and usable. Generally speaking, students notice improvement in fitness, coordination, and self-defense skills very quickly. Within three months of regular class attendance and practice, most students feel better, operate with more mental acuity, and feel many times more confident with their ability to defend themselves in a self-defense encounter.

True proficiency at karate, however, is usually defined as the point of mastery of basic techniques and achieving a workable understanding of principles, strategies, and philosophies. This proficiency comes much later, usually four to six years, and is generally acknowledged by awarding the rank of black belt. (In many Chinese styles this award is a black sash rather than a belt.)

So true proficiency, in the usual sense of the word, takes a while. But you can begin now to achieve many of the benefits that initially attracted you to the art. Ultimate progress is limited only by the amount of time and energy you decide to put into your study of the martial arts.

WHAT ABOUT THE BELT RANKING SYSTEM? WHAT DO DIFFERENT COLORED BELTS MEAN AND WHEN ARE THEY AWARDED?

Colored belts are traditionally awarded in the martial arts to indicate a student's level of proficiency. This is important during class when one student may want to seek out another for assistance. Japanese, Okinawan, and Korean styles award belts, while many Chinese styles use sashes. Each colored belt or sash corresponds to a number that indicates, in a decreasing fashion, how far the student is from the rank of black belk or black sash. The following chart shows the commonly-used belt colors in the Japanese, Okinawan, and Korean styles, and how they correspond to the number ranking system. Also shown is the length of time usually required from a student's starting point to each rank, although this varies depending upon the instructor and the student's aptitude. It should also be noted that the Chinese arts usually use fewer ranks and longer time periods between each rank.

GENERAL RANKING SYSTEM: JAPANESE, OKINAWAN, KOREAN KARATE

Number Rank	Belt Color	Time to Achieve
10th Student Grade	White	Novice
9th Student Grade	White	Novice
8th Student Grade	White or yellow (gold)	1-2 mos.
7th Student Grade	Yellow (gold) or orange	2-4 mos.
6th Student Grade	Blue, green or purple	4-6 mos.
5th Student Grade	Blue, green or purple	6-10 mos.
4th Student Grade	Blue, green or purple	10-14 mos.
3rd Student Grade	Brown or red	15 mos.-2 yrs.
2nd Student Grade	Brown or red	15 mos.-2 yrs.
1st Student Grade	Brown or red	2-3 yrs.
1st Instructor Level	Black	3½-5 yrs.
2nd Instructor Level	Black	5-7 yrs.
3rd Instructor Level	Black	7-10 yrs.
4th Instructor Level	Black or red/white	10-14 yrs.
5th Instructor Level	Black or red/white	14-18 yrs.
6th Instructor Level	Black, red/white or black/red	18-22 yrs.
7th Instructor Level	Black, red/white or black/red	22-30 yrs.
8th Instructor Level	Black, red/white or black/red	Over 30 yrs.
9th Instructor Level	Black, red/white or black/red	Over 30 yrs.-2nd only to style leader
10th Instructor Level	Black, black/red or red	Leader of Style

HOW DO I ADVANCE FROM RANK TO RANK? AND HOW DO I KNOW WHEN I AM READY TO ADVANCE?

Usually a test is given (written, skills, or both) to determine the student's qualifications for each rank, although non-test "spot" promotions are infrequently given for outstanding progress or accomplishment. Generally a "Certificate of Rank," suitable for framing, is awarded with each belt, and bears the name of the instructor and school authorizing and awarding the rank.

The difficulty of the tests increases proportionately to the increase in the level of rank being tested for. Since the student is always testing for a rank he or she has not yet achieved, the decision to test is either left entirely to the instructor, or the student may make the decision based on guidelines and criteria established by the instructor.

AT WHAT POINT WILL I BE CONSIDERED AN "ADVANCED" KARATE STUDENT?

The usual separation point between a beginning student and one who has become an "advanced beginner" is the award of the first or second belt (usually two to four months). The "intermediate" stage is reached with the earning of the second or third belt (four to ten months). A student is referred to as "advanced" when he or she earns the fifth or sixth belt grade (usually this corresponds to three grades away from black belt). This belt color is usually red or brown.

Of course, the belt color is only an outward symbol of the true reason a student is considered "beginner," "intermediate," or "advanced." The knowledge and experience the student has gained, along with loyalty, enthusiasm, and desire to learn more, are the real signs that a student has "matured" in the martial arts, or has become an "advanced" pupil. Remember that although technical ability is important, it is not as important to your instructor as attitude, dedication, and the desire to gain (and pass on) increasingly greater quantities of martial arts knowledge.

DOES FORMAL KARATE TRAINING STOP AT THE BLACK BELT LEVEL?

Far from it. In fact, it has been said that karate training really begins at the level of black belt. Of course, much training occurs before this, but the figurative idea is that the time spent prior to black belt is much like an individual's formal schooling before college — the basics of generalized education are in preparation for entry into an institution of higher learning. Similarly, the time a student spends before black belt is spent conditioning body and forming a mental attitude, cultivating positive thought processes, neutralizing frustration and discouragement, and forging determination. A great deal of this training comes during the advanced student stages, a year or so before the black belt promotion, and occurs as a result of the student's participation as an assistant instructor. Disseminating information and answering questions usually reveals and helps correct any lack of knowledge of inadequacies.

I HAVE HEARD OF DIFFERENT KARATE STYLES BEING CLASSIFIED AS "SOFT" OR "HARD." WHAT DOES THIS MEAN?

The term "soft" and "hard" are commonly used to differentiate those styles preferring circular, non-striking blocks from those utilizing striking blocks. The former usually refers to the styles of Chinese origin, while the latter generally indicates an Okinawan, Japanese, or Korean style. These terms are actually somewhat misleading, since the "soft" styles also have striking blocks in their repertoire, and the "hard" styles often practice circular, non-striking blocks. "Soft" and "hard" styles do not refer to the strikes used by the various styles. The actual fighting tactics and strategies used by the two classifications are similar (and are becoming even more similar as a result of new styles emerging from open sport karate competition). Today, the terms "soft" and "hard" are primarily used to categorize traditional martial arts forms (choreographed fighting patterns against imaginary opponents) for purposes of competition.

ARE SOME STYLES MORE SUITABLE FOR COMPETITION THAN OTHERS?

None of the traditional styles of karate were intended, during their development, to be used for competition (with the possible exception of some Korean styles which have emerged since karate competition in Korea became popular). Many traditional styles have been adapted by their instructors, however, to increase the effectiveness of the style in modern open karate competitions. We would then say that these instructors have taken a "contemporary" approach to their style and the way that they teach it, with regard to modern sport karate ideologies. This does not mean these instructors have lost, for their students, the traditional benefits of their style nor the self-defense advantages; rather, they have added to their teachings new discoveries and concepts. The program they teach is therefore more complete and their students benefit, whether or not they compete.

The only styles which are naturally more suitable for competition than others are those that have recently come into being solely for the purpose of training karate competitors. Most of these styles, however, sacrifice training in form and self-defense for increased time spent on sport concepts.

WHICH STYLE IS THE BEST? HOW DO I KNOW WHICH ONE IS RIGHT FOR ME?

No one style is better than any of the others. There are literally hundreds of bona fide karate styles worldwide, and nearly all have been developed for the primary purposes of self-defense, fitness, and self-development. What makes a style more suitable for one person or another is not really the elements of the style, but the approach taken by the instructor and the areas of the style emphasized. If the instructor does not touch on the sport aspects and you are interested in competition, you may be happier in a different class. If your interest leans more to just staying in good condition, you will want to attend workouts that do not emphasize competition over fitness.

Ideally, the karate program with which you become involved should be well-rounded, and the instructor should have a working knowledge of the various aspects of his or her style and how to help students get what they want from their training. Realistically, as a beginner, you know very little about the art you have chosen to study and thus have little information or experience by which to judge the quality of your instructor. However, you should know after a month or so of classes whether or not the program you are enrolled in is meeting your needs and keeping your interest. If not, you may want to examine another program. Even if the new program is the same style, the emphasis may be different because of a different instructor. Just make sure you give one program a chance before moving to another.

ARE THERE ANY DIFFERENCES BETWEEN MEN AND WOMEN WHEN IT COMES TO LEARNING KARATE SKILLS?

Men and women appear to learn the actual skills of execution at an equal rate. When there does appear to be a general difference, however, is in obtaining the physical capacity to execute those skills effectively.

Women are certainly as physically coordinated as men, and in many cases they find karate movements easier to execute initially. Most women are more flexible in the hips and hamstrings than males and thus have an easier time with certain stances and kicking techniques.

Men, however, hold the edge in natural strength. Their ratio of muscular mass to body weight is normally higher than females, and this brings an advantage in speed and power.

Generally, men seem to react better to the mental implication of an art having potential for violence. The past decade has seen some shift in the attitude of women toward self-defense. As violent attacks on women have increased in frequency, many females have accepted the need to learn to defend themselves. This new awareness adds increased determination and purpose to a woman's study of the martial arts, and assists in overcoming any differences in strength and body mass between male and female practitioners.

HOW FLEXIBLE CAN I BECOME FROM MY KARATE WORKOUTS?

The answer to this question really lies in two factors: first, you will become as flexible as genetic and structural factors allow; and second, you will approach this potential in direct proportion to the amount of time and frequency applied to proper stretching exercises. Note the use of the word "proper," for as you will see in Chapter 6, there are definite right and wrong ways to stretch. Before you panic on "genetic and structural" flexibility limitation, be assured that nearly everyone possesses enough natural flexibility to execute effectively most martial arts techniques, *if* that potential flexibility is developed in the proper manner.

WILL WEIGHT TRAINING HELP OR HURT MY KARATE?

It depends entirely on which weight training exercises you do and how you do them.

You will find that executing karate techniques forces you to use most of the muscles in your body. A properly supervised program of strength training that works the major muscle groups of the upper and lower body can be very helpful to you and your karate, if you follow these principles:

1. Stronger muscles, generally speaking, will allow you to execute your karate techniques more quickly and with more power. Therefore, the muscle groups that produce the karate movements are the ones to emphasize in your weight training. These include the calves, quadriceps, and hamstrings of the legs; hips and buttock muscles; abdominals and obliques; chest, shoulders, and back; and the forearm and upper-arm muscles. Other body muscles may, of course, be exercised, but if your time is limited, concentrate on those needed the most to help advance the skills you have chosen to learn.

2. Choose strength training equipment that will give you the safest, most efficient results for time spent. Many brands of weight machines have become popular in recent years, and generally these devices follow sound principles and produce good results. Look for a machine or set of machines that will deliver a varying resistance to the muscle as you perform the exercise, and will exercise the muscle throughout its full normal range of movement. Barbells continue to be widely used, but it is usually more difficult to attain this varying resistance and full-range movement with "free" weights than with machines. Also, free weights can often be less safe than machines, and they should always be used with close supervision.

3. Do *not* attempt to isolate and work those muscles used most for karate by simulating a karate movement with added weight.

A common, and damaging, misconception in many sports is that if the body motion involved in the skill of the sport can be reproduced under greater load during weight training, then the body will "think" that load is still there when the skill is performed during actual competition, thereby producing faster movements. (An example can be seen in the baseball player who swings a lead bat just before going to the plate.) In reality, it doesn't work that way. What actually happens is that the muscles may derive some strengthening benefit, but at the cost of confusing the body's motor mechanisms. Any skill (such as swinging a bat to hit a baseball) usually involves timing and precision, and must be practiced under the same conditions, time after time, and under the *same conditions that will be experienced during competition.* Attempting to practice otherwise will only damage the precise timing and focus needed for a particular athletic skill (i.e., the baseball player should swing a lead bat only if he or she plans to actually go to the plate during the game with that bat).

So be sure not to mix your strength and skill work. Avoid kicking with ankle weights, or blocking with hand weights.

4. Arrange a proper schedule for your weight workouts and stick to it. The best time to do your strength work is after your karate workouts, not before. Your karate practice should concentrate primarily on skill work. This skill work, including the number of repetitions of any technique that can be properly performed, will suffer significantly if it takes place too soon after a strength workout. Fully exhausted muscles do not perform precision movements well. *After* your karate practice, however, your muscles will be loose, warmed-up, and slightly pre-exhausted. Weight training at this time is very productive.

For best results establish a regular training schedule, since the time between strength workouts is very important. Also, remember your strength will increase much faster than your recovery ability. Three times a week is a good schedule to begin with, but stick with one day's rest between each session. Otherwise, you may find yourself decreasing in strength, rather than increasing, due to overtraining. Additionally, as your strength increases you may need additional recovery time.

More information on specific strength training exercises and theories may be found in the book, *Weight Training Everyone* (Tuten, Moore, and Knight, Hunter Textbooks, Inc., Winston-Salem, N.C., 1982).

WHAT ABOUT THE BODY CONDITIONING, OR HARDENING, THAT I'VE HEARD STORIES ABOUT?

Usually these tales refer to the "hardening" of certain areas of the body to withstand impact from striking or being struck. This is commonly seen in the calloused knuckles, feet, or shins of the martial artist who specializes in breaking hard objects such as boards or bricks, and is generally accomplished through repeatedly striking hard objects with increasing force over a period of time.

It cannot be emphasized enough that it is not necessary to practice such body-callousing in order to become a skilled and effective practitioner. Even if breaking demonstrations are desired, the martial artist can always use a naturally-padded striking surface, such as the knife-hand, palm-heel, or ball of the foot, rather than callousing bony surfaces. Certainly it is not necessary for self-defense; in all likelihood it will not be included in a generalized karate class.

The type of body conditioning that *should* be included is the kind already discussed — training the muscles and joints for both strength and suppleness to facilitate execution of technique and to help withstand any attacks that the martial artist may be unfortunate enough to experience.

HOW MUCH TIME SHOULD I DEVOTE TO KARATE WORKOUTS?

The length of time you will spend actually working out in karate will vary as your involvement progresses. As a beginning student, you will gain the most benefit by attending three or four classes each week, preferably spaced a day apart, with no more than two classes every three days. The off-days should include a brief stretching session sometime during the day or even two such sessions, perhaps morning and evening. Light stretching is hard to overdo. By contrast, however, taxing physical workouts should be spaced throughout the week. In this case, more does not mean *better*. Many karate students have unknowingly hindered their progress by overtraining. Too much too often can bring you *less* in the long run, and this becomes even more likely to happen as you become better trained. As you become conditioned and know more techniques to practice, you may find your workouts getting longer, particularly those you regulate yourself, as opposed to a class situation. When this happens (usually after three or five months for the dedicated student), you should reduce your hard workouts to three a week and closely monitor the length of time you spend in each workout. The experienced martial artist will stay busy during his or her training time, and gain maximum benefit for time spent.

In summary, we can say that as a student acquires better conditioning and learns more, the length of workouts should increase by 50% or less, but the intensity of those workouts may triple or quadruple. In addition, the number of sessions per week may even decrease, as the heightened intensity of these workouts will demand a greater amount of recovery time between them.

HOW SHOULD I PRACTICE ON MY OWN?

The first thing to do is to become mentally motivated. Decide exactly how long you will work out and what you will practice. Tell yourself that this workout will make you one workout better than yesterday, and one workout closer to your goal of becoming a proficient martial artist. You should ask your instructor about your weaknesses, and be sure to work on these in your session. Also, include new techniques you have been learning, and others you know and like to practice. If you can secure a partner to practice with, do kicking drills with one another and critique, to the best of your knowledge, one another's technique. Don't overdo the length of your workout. Anything longer than 90 minutes means you've got too much nonworking time during your session — you should be tired within 90 minutes. Never train hard, particularly during hot weather, without taking a short break every 20-30 minutes or less. Continuing to practice repetitiously a technique after fatigue has solidly set in only means you are practicing to do the technique

wrong, and you should take a short rest or switch to another technique that uses a body part that is not fatigued. Water or a formulated thirst-quencher should always be readily available at your workout site, and you should partake frequently, even if you don't feel very thirsty. If you are perspiring, you are losing water, and your performance will quickly suffer unless you replace it. Finally, keep safety in mind. Don't try a new technique that you don't feel confident with if there is any risk involved, and be sure to warm up properly before you get started. Be particularly cautious if you are training alone. Most injuries become more severe if treatment if delayed; if you are working out alone and injure yourself, you may not receive treatment as quickly as you might otherwise.

IS THERE A SPECIAL BREATHING PATTERN I SHOULD FOLLOW WHILE WORKING OUT?

Yes there is, and it is extremely important. The karate techniques you will learn include punches, kicks, blocks, and body movements. The speed with which you execute these moves and the effectiveness of your strikes and blocks is increased by breathing out, rapidly, upon execution. An inward breath at these times will actually slow your techniques and reactions. Inward breaths should be through the nose, and occur during the periods of momentary relaxation between executions. Outward breaths should be through the nose or mouth, and should involve not only the lungs and normal breathing mechanisms, but also the abdominal muscles. These muscles should squeeze inward as they tighten, helping to force air from the lungs in a rapid rush timed to coincide precisely with the impact moment of the techniques, be they strikes or blocks. A greater degree of muscular contraction will result, creating a faster and more powerful technique. You should also strive to allow the contraction to involve other major body muscles as well, including the back, legs, and buttocks. This will create a strong foundation for the technique and eliminate weak body links that could act as unwanted shock absorbers for the impact of your techniques — an impact that you want the target to absorb. You will then be better able to absorb a counterstrike without injury.

WHAT ABOUT THE YELL I HAVE HEARD FROM MARTIAL ARTISTS AS THEY EXECUTE A TECHNIQUE? IS IT NECESSARY?

The loud noise which often accompanies a martial artist's technique is referred to as a "kiai" (KEY-eye) in Japanese, or "kihup" (KEY-up) in Korean. There is no literal English translation, so for literary simplicity we will call it a "kiai."

The timing, purposes, and advantages of the outward breath coinciding with the execution of techniques have already been discussed. When a martial artist uses a kiai, he or she follows this same breathing pattern but increases the effectiveness even further by combining it with a loud vocal sound. The origin point of this sound is the center abdominal area (the same muscles used in singing), and its primary purpose is to intensify mental concentration and its link to physical exertion. The desired result is the collection and release of a maximum of speed and power in the technique. (For a further explanation of kiais, see Chapter 8.)

ISN'T KARATE DANGEROUS? CAN'T I GET HURT TRAINING OR SPARRING WITH THE OTHER STUDENTS?

Any athletic activity has certain risks of injury and the human mind will always seek to overcome those limitations. The notion that karate is more dangerous than other activities is entirely untrue.

Certainly karate can be quite dangerous if practiced with malintent; however, properly conducted karate classes stress just the opposite — a genuine concern and respect for the well-being of fellow students and an acceptance of the personal responsibility that accompanies the knowledge of effective self-defense.

Sparring is the area of training in which most bodily contact occurs, and therefore has the greatest potential for one student to injure another. However, students do not progress into sparring practice until they exhibit adequate control over their techniques to prevent striking their sparring partner (if sparring without safety equipment is allowed by the instructor), or to prevent striking their partner too hard (if safety equipment is used). A skilled instructor will know how to help students keep their natural emotional responses to sparring (such as fear, frustration, or possibly even anger) under control, and prevent these responses from upsetting the atmosphere of safety and progress that should surround a sparring session. With a good teacher, well informed students, and proper policies and rules, karate training and sparring should be much less dangerous than most activities involving student-student interaction.

WHEN DO I START COMPETING IN KARATE AND WHAT IS AVAILABLE TO ME?

You never *have* to compete in karate and, in fact, most students never do. Competition does have several good points, however, including the experience of sparring with new opponents, learning to handle a pressure situation, and the development of sportsmanship. The type of competition recommended for most students is the light-contact version popular throughout the United States and Canada, or the non-contact version prevalent in the Orient and many Asian and European countries.

In **light-contact** competition, specially-designed, padded gloves and boots are worn, as well as protective mouth, shin, and groin guards (for men). Contestants are allowed to make only light contact with their strikes, and each technique that shows proper focus to a vital target area gains the executing contestant one point toward a winning score. Hard contact that could cause injury brings a penalty. Techniques such as elbow, knee, and finger strikes are not allowed (see the Appendix for complete detail on light-contact competition rules). The light-contact version of sport karate is relatively new, coming into being with the invention of the hand and foot padded gear, or "safety equipment," in 1974, and is the fastest-growing version.

Non-contact karate, the first version of the sport to be developed, came into being in a small way in the Orient in the late 1930s or early 1940s. Its present form is similar to the original version, with very little safety equipment being allowed, and contestants are expected to stop all techniques to the head just short of contact (some Korean and Chinese factions do allow head contact with kicks), since the hands and feet have little or no padding attached. This type of competition has gained much disfavor in North America due to safety considerations, and relatively few American tournaments now follow these rules.

In addition to these types of **sparring** competition, most tournaments also include **forms** competition, in which contestants perform choreographed fighting demonstrations indicative of their respective styles and are judged by a panel of qualified officials (much like a gymnastics, skating or diving competition).

So which competition is right for you, should you decide to try it? Anyone who has learned a form, even the new student, can enter forms competition. Sparring competition may begin as soon as your instructor feels you have learned enough to benefit from the experience. The light-contact version is recommended over the non-contact variety; the non-contact type of event should be approached with caution, as the lack of safety equipment leaves your safety in the hands of your opponent and the officials' ability to enforce the rules. Enter this type of competition only if your instructor strongly recommends it.

One more word about competition. If you choose to compete, all well-organized tournaments will have a suitable number of divisions for competitors, so you would be sparring with, or running your form against, other martial artists of your rank and level of experience. You will also be very nervous at your first competition, and will feel some apprehension and anxiety each time you enter one. Just keep in mind that this is normal with any competitive event that you wish to do well in, and the experience can help you learn to control excess apprehension and turn it to your advantage. Whether or not you are ready for the experience or competition is best known by your instructor, and he or she should be consulted before entering an event.

WHY DO I NEED TO WEAR THE TRADITIONAL UNIFORM TO LEARN KARATE?

You don't need to wear it in order to learn karate. And you certainly don't have to have one on to be able to utilize what you know. However, your instructor may request, with good reason, that you wear one during practice.

The uniform may be one of two general types. The standard Japanese, Korean, or Okinawan uniform consists of loose-fitting pants held in place by a drawstring, laces or elastic. The top is a loose-fitting jacket, which crosses in the front and stays that way with ties located on each side. The Chinese style of uniform is similar except the jacket is held together in the front by a different method. An instructor may modify the student's uniform because of personal preferences, such as requiring a certain color, rolled-up or short sleeves, tee-shirt instead of jackets, etc. (See Chapter 4 for more details on uniforms and belts.) What each of these uniforms has in common, however, is that they are designed for the type of activity the student will be undertaking. The long, loose pants will help keep the leg muscles warm while allowing for maximum movement during stretching and kicking, and the jacket does the same for the muscles of the upper body.

The uniform also has important psychological training advantages. It becomes a symbol of the student's dedication to the art of karate and his or her own self-discipline. Putting on the uniform means that it's time to practice karate, both physically and mentally. Many activities are undertaken in street clothes or running suits, but the karate uniform is suitable only for karate. Wearing the uniform becomes an outward sign of the student's commitment to the practice, and ultimate mastery, of the martial arts. It follows that this effect is magnified if everyone in the class is in a similar uniform. Students showing a common style of dress share common goals and dedication, since the uniform is a symbol of that dedication. Group spirit, obtained in this manner and in other ways, is one of the most important factors in maintaining and increasing the productiveness of a karate class. The uniform may not literally be necessary for a student to learn karate, but most instructors believe it enables their students to learn in the most effective and efficient manner. For most students, it is an important factor in their mental approach to the study of the martial arts, as well as in creating a proper physical environment.

세계 태권도 협회

空手 柔道 統神拳

HOW MUCH ORIENTAL LANGUAGE MUST I LEARN AND WHY?

The primary reason for learning some Oriental terminology is to maintain a link with the traditional origins of the art. Many students, particularly as they delve deeper into a particular chosen style, develop an increasing interest in the historic beginnings of their art, and appreciate links with that past, such as the use of traditional Oriental names for techniques, the uniform and training area, or the numbers for counting.

Another reason for learning some Oriental terminology is to allow easy communication between instructors and students of different countries and languages. This is important for widespread styles, particularly those with strong Oriental ties. A student well-versed in traditional terminology may study with instructors in Europe, Asia, or the Orient, with much less language difficulty, so long as those instructors maintain some knowledge of the traditional language of the art.

Some instructors may not feel the need to teach or use traditional terminology. Some may use the traditional names only when identifying forms, while others may do almost all of their teaching in an Oriental or other traditional language. The Japanese, Korean, and Okinawan styles are most likely to require some use of traditional language; the Chinese, Thai, Vietnamese and Burmese styles generally use less vocabulary, probably because of the greater pronunciation problems encountered with these languages by Caucasians. American styles will seldom use Oriental terms, and then only for the traditional forms which they retain within the style.

WHY IS THERE SO MUCH BOWING?

Again, we are speaking of traditional customs, but this custom has a purpose of utmost importance.

Bowing is a physical act that helps develop, demonstrate and maintain instructor-student and student-student respect, a respect which will hopefully be transferred to all fellow persons encountered in the student's daily life. Each time students bow to their instructor, they are demonstrating a recognition of that instructor's capabilities and good intentions, and their respect and gratitude toward that instructor. Each time students bow to one another, they are exhibiting recognition of one another as fellow persons with a common goal of physical and mental advancement, as opposed to men and women learning to just be "fighting machines." The same statements are made at other times in our lives, with handshakes, verbal salutes, or physical salutes to the flag or military officers. Bowing is the way to show this same feeling with martial artists.

HOW EFFECTIVE IS KARATE AS A MEANS OF SELF-DEFENSE, WITH RELATIVELY EASY ACCESS TO GUNS AND OTHER WEAPONS?

The question is most easily answered by asking several others: Do you own a gun or fighting knife? If so, do you carry it on your person at all times? And even if you do, are you prepared to use it against an unarmed opponent?

Few people own or carry fighting knives. Those who do own guns usually don't carry them on their person, as it is seldom desirable or legal to do so. And while displaying a deadly weapon may scare off an attacker, what if it doesn't? Using deadly force against an unarmed attacker, even if within your moral margins, is legal only under specific circumstances. Generally speaking, you must show not only that you were in danger of being assaulted, but were in reasonable fear for your life. That may be difficult to prove with an unarmed assailant. And if you **don't** use your weapon against the attacker, there is always a chance the attacker may overpower you and use your weapon on *you*.

Obviously a gun or knife is an excellent self-defense tool; the point is that such weapons, when used, are basically all-or-nothing, and leave little room for error or half-way measures. They are really meant for truly life-threatening encounters, certainly not for the drunk who won't let go of your arm when you refuse to dance or the irate driver who takes a swing at you over a minor traffic accident. Perhaps the most obvious advantage of unarmed expertise over weapons is that any gun, knife, or club keeps you safe only if you carry it with you at all times, and can use it before your attacker nails you first.

By contrast, your karate never gets lost, stuck in a holster, misfires, nor can it be used against you. As long as you maintain your skills and reflexes through practice, you are prepared to deflect or avoid a first attack, and deliver your own counterstrike. Or you can execute a disarming and/or incapacitating technique, inflicting only minor damage on your assailant. In short, you possess constant readiness and more options.

Chapter 3
Equipment and Facilities

The Uniform and Belt

The uniform selected by your instructor will be suited for the particular type of activity you will be doing. It will permit easy movement, and keep deep vital muscle areas covered and warm during workouts. Several of the most popular types of uniforms are described below. All are suitable for use by both males and females.

Japanese, Okinawan, Korean, or Chinese Kempo Traditional Uniform. The top fastens with ties; pants with a drawstring. American styles also generally use this type of uniform. Some Korean styles add a colored lapel and seam trim to match the student's belt color. White or black are the usual colors, although other colors have come into increasing use in recent years.

Contemporary competition-style Uniform. The top is cut short and fastens in the front with velcro. (This kind of top is sometimes replaced by the more traditional type seen below.) Pants are of the "lace-up" (shown) or "all elastic" variety. Colors vary; stripes are often seen on both pants and top.

Equipment and Facilities

Traditional Chinese Kung-Fu Uniform. The top fastens with small loops, pants are of the all elastic variety. The uniform is almost always black with white trim. The top is sometimes replaced with a black tee-shirt. A sash is worn rather than a belt.

Any of several methods of tying the belt may be used. One of the more popular methods is shown below:

STEP 1: Start with the belt passing behind you, one end pressed against your waist with your right hand, and the left hand holding the slack.

STEP 2: Circle your waist with the belt, laying the belt flat on top of itself all the way around. Be sure there are no twists in it. Pull the end you originally had placed against you out from underneath.

STEP 3: Slide the belt around your waist until the two ends are equal in length.

STEP 4: Pass the end on top *underneath* both belt layers (working upwards), and back out the top.

STEP 5: Make a loop with this "top end" and pass the "bottom" end over and through the loop.

STEP 6: Grasp one end in each hand and PULL!

IMPROPER TIE: Ends extend upward and downward. Repeat steps 4 through 6.

PROPER TIE: Both ends are equal and extend to sides and down.

Striking Bags

Striking bags can be useful training aids if used consistently and correctly. The most important thing to remember when using training bags is that the object is not just to strike the bag hard, but rather to use *proper technique* on the bag, which should result in a solid hit. Some bags are for power building and others are for coordination and speed, but all follow this basic idea.

Learning to use a striking bag properly takes time, and can only be accomplished through the help of your instructor. Several of the most popular types of training bags are illustrated below.

SPEED BAG. Attached to a wooden backboard by a universal swivel, the speed bag is designed to build hand speed and hand-eye coordination. It is alternately struck by either hand, with a quick rebound requiring hand speed and timing.

Equipment and Facilities

HEAVY BAG. Usually hung from the ceiling by a chain, the heavy bag weighs 60-80 pounds and provides a weighty yet resilient target for hand techniques and kicks.

MEDIUM BAG. Similar in design to the heavy bag, the medium bag is usually only 30-40 pounds, and is made to "move" more when struck, mimicking more closely the movement of an opponent. It is particularly useful for jabbing hand techniques and head kicks.

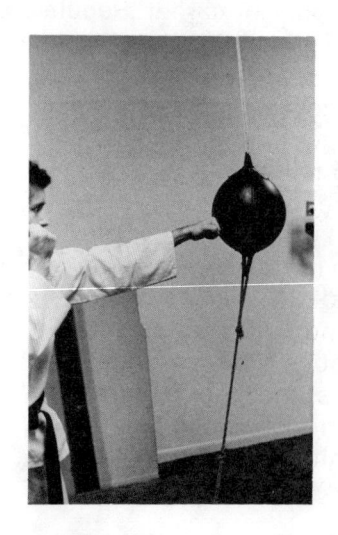

DOUBLE-END BAG. Attached to both floor and ceiling, the double-end bag provides realistic movement for hand techniques and the lighter kicks.

AIR BAG. The air bag is an excellent training tool for developing power kicks. One person holds the bag and moves backward slightly with each kick, while the kicker concentrates on front, side, round, back and spin kicks. An air valve allows for adjustable absorbency.

HAND TARGETS. Not really a bag, hand targets are made of foam rubber and are useful for speed kicks and hand techniques. Partner holds one on each hand, moving them in the manner of an opponent.

Workout Floor and Mirrors

The ideal area for general karate work is a relatively large, open space with good lighting and ventilation. Karate can be practiced anywhere, but a square or rectangular workout room of about a thousand square feet or more allows for free movement by several persons or a small class. The floor should be any slightly resilient material, such as polished wood, Tartan, rubber or carpet. Regular practice on floors that are too hard, such as tile or concrete, will be hard on the feet and legs, and should be avoided. Likewise, surfaces that are too soft, such as plush carpeting, or outdoor sites such as a sand beach will require you to spend too much time trying to stay stable in your stances, and are not suitable for regular training.

One of the most valuable training aids the martial artist can take advantage of is a mirror. Once the student knows what a particular technique is supposed to look like, the mirror provides an invaluable way to achieve unassisted, immediate feedback.

Make mirror work a regular part of your nonclass training. Move toward the mirror while executing techniques slow and fast, and look for errors in body or limb placement, stances, or accuracy of strikes. Practice your forms a step at a time, checking each body position and stance. Mirrors should be positioned so you can view your entire body from four to six feet away.

Equipment and Facilities

WORKOUT FLOOR: A 1400 square foot workout area with carpet flooring.

MIRRORS: Self-examination of a form using wall mirrors.

Stretching Aids

Generally speaking, you don't need anything to assist in stretching except time and desire. *Consistency, correct technique* and *patience* are the real key to achieving flexibility, and most students will find the great majority of their stretching is done alone and unassisted. Because stretching needs to be done frequently, it is not always possible to have a partner or a stretching aid. However, several tools, when available, can assist you in achieving your flexibility goals. (Partner stretching will be covered in Chapter 6.)

Stretching bars are one of the best aids possible and have been used for decades by dancers. Start with a bar that isn't too high for you; if you have to "kick" your leg up to get it over the bar, it's probably too high. Pick a height at which your leg feels the stretch, but no real pain, and relax until the stretching sensation is gone. Then go to a slightly higher bar, or bend your body toward your leg to intensify the stretch.

36   Equipment and Facilities

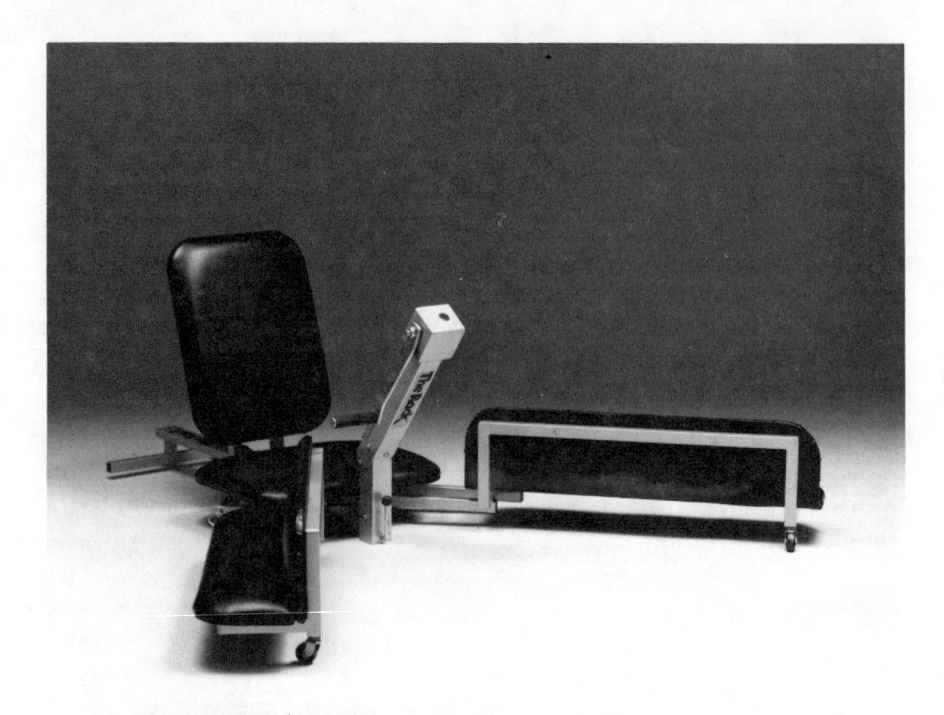

Another good stretching tool, this one for the lateral (sideways) stretch, is a mechanical device known as a **stretch rack.** A hand cranked lever slowly moves the legs of the machine apart, moving your legs apart. Again, be careful not to overstretch. Flexibility takes patience and time, not the ability to withstand pain.

Other stretching aids include such simple devices as a rope or belt with a loop flung over a ceiling beam, and new ones are constantly being developed. Caution should always be exercised when trying a new method, and a good general rule is to stay away from any device or stretching method that doesn't keep you feeling as though you have complete control over the amount of stretch you are receiving at any given time.

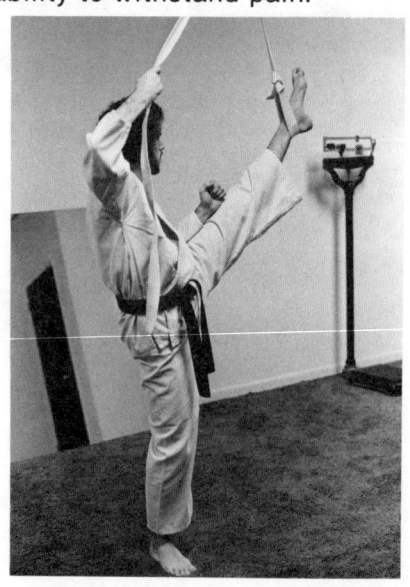

Miscellaneous Equipment

An often overlooked, but very valuable aid to a martial artist's conditioning, is the **jump rope.** Benefits include stamina and leg strength (especially in the ankles and calves), and regular use will show definite development of footwork and mobility. The ideal rope is the leather and ball-bearing type, although a plastic chip or nylon rope will suffice. Lengths vary between six and ten feet, with the average-sized man needing an eight-footer, and the average woman a seven-foot rope.

Bag gloves are useful for the martial artist who spends time with the striking bags. These bags are usually vinyl, leather, or canvas covered, and bag gloves help protect against skin abrasion and callous buildups. Bag gloves are generally of vinyl or leather (with vinyl being the more economical and more durable), and are classified by quality and weight.

(Sparring gear and weight training equipment will be covered in subsequent chapters.)

CHAPTER 3 EVALUATION

Multiple Choice: Circle the letter of the best answer.

1. The type of uniform you will be wearing in your karate class will be determined by:
   a. the style of karate you will be studying
   b. your preference
   c. your instructor's preference
   d. whatever is "on sale" at the time

2. The most important thing to remember when using a striking bag is:
   a. to follow a short-duration workout
   b. to use proper technique
   c. to hit the bag HARD!
   d. to hit the bag softy, but with *rhythm*

3. The speed bag is designed to:
   a. help you hit harder
   b. help you kick faster
   c. frustrate you!
   d. build hand speed

4. The best bags for developing power kicks should be the:
   a. heavy bag and air bag
   b. speed bag and air bag
   c. double end bag, air bag, and paper bag
   d. heavy bag and hand targets

5. Benefits obtainable with consistent use of the jump rope include:
   a. stamina
   b. footwork and mobility
   c. leg strength
   d. all of the above

Fill in the blanks:

1. The type of uniform that includes a short, velcro fastening top is generally referred to as _____ dress.

2. The heavy bag is usually hung from a beam or the ceiling, and generally weighs _____ pounds.

3. Your workout floor for karate should be of a slightly resilient material such as _____, rather than a hard substance such as _____.

Equipment and Facilities

4. Wall mirrors should be positioned so that you can see _____ while standing four to six feet away.

5. The real keys to achieving flexibility are _____, _____, _____.

Chapter 4
The Mental Aspect

Basic Philosophy

Karate is a fighting art. Make no mistake about it — by its very definition as a martial art, karate is based on confrontation with opponents. In a physical sense, karate is designed to be the ultimate in unarmed self-defense: a method that uses all parts of the body for blocking and striking, and incorporates sophisticated techniques for avoiding attacks, maneuvering opponents, and maximizing destructive power within certain techniques.

But in a non-physical sense, karate is more than this. Much more! The training of the body is only an outward sign of the inward discipline of the karate student. Through years of training, the mind, like the body, becomes both hard and supple: self-defense capability is in strong evidence, but the mind also shows a softer side. A new appreciation is there for the destructive powers we all possess, and how they can, with proper timing, be used to harm one another. It is a fact that the true follower of karate will increase his or her physical potential year by year, but actually become less likely, as those years pass, to ever want or need to use that potential against another person. With ability comes confidence — often enough in itself to discourage a would-be assailant. And with confidence comes serenity — it is no longer necessary to prove to oneself or to others that one's skills are adequate. It becomes enough to appreciate karate for its pleasures of conditioning, discipline, or sport. The student who has trained hard has benefitted both physically and mentally and is content in that knowledge.

Karate cannot produce discipline in an individual; instead karate helps the individual develop *self*-discipline — the discipline that stimulates a person to achieve his or her goals no matter what obstacles lie in wait. Laziness, procrastination, discouragement — all can be conquered by the self-discipline within us that karate training can awaken and show us how to use and develop. In short, we become winners — not just on belt ranking tests or in martial arts tournaments, but in contests against our weaker selves and in our lives as a whole.

Karate has no central philosophy other than the ancient code of ethics that admonishes the student always to do his or her best, to be humble, and always to use karate for good. The real philosophy of the martial arts, the real benefit, is what it teaches us about ourselves — our strengths and our weaknesses, learning to accept temporary defeat along with triumph, conquering doubt and discouragement with understanding of the art and ourselves, acquiring positive results in anything through discipline and positive thinking. The only absolutely forbidden words within a martial arts school are "I can't." Those words are an acceptance, not of reality, but of hopelessness — the surety of failure due to negative attitude. In the words of one of the greatest of karate masters, Hironori Otsuka, "The difference between the impossible and the possible is one's will." The true follower of the martial arts knows this to be true.

Developing Self-discipline and Good Training Habits

Laziness is a trait that no one has a monopoly on. Along with the discipline within us, laziness is waiting for a chance to show us the easy way out. Beating that laziness isn't easy but it can be done, and proper karate training shows you how.

First, impress firmly into your mind the positive benefits of being a disciplined person (and be assured the discipline you develop for your karate training *will* carry over into other areas of your life). Think of the pride you will have in yourself, and others will have for you, once you reach your goals of self-discipline.

As you progress in karate rank, you have an added responsibility of self-discipline and good training habits, since all the lower ranks look to you as an example! So set a definite goal for yourself. Make a workout/class attendance schedule and stick to it. If you pull a muscle and can't kick for one or two workouts with your left leg, substitute more right-leg kicks and hand techniques. Don't make excuses! They won't get you anything you really want. Each workout you miss puts you, forevermore, one workout behind where you could have been.

During your actual training, strive to get the most results for your time. When in class, go full speed throughout, unless directed otherwise. Always put out one hundred percent and concentrate mentally. Don't let your mind wander to other things. Make perfection your goal and strive to come closer with each workout. Become fascinated with how fast you can execute your backfist or roundhouse kick, or how much power you can get in your reverse punch or sidekick. Pick out one of the senior students, watch his or her technique and attitude, and use it as an example. Be the best you can be and make up your mind you'll never settle for less. When doing drills or repetitions, never just count numbers. Always try to make each technique a little faster, stronger, or more accurate than the last one.

Defeating Discouragement

As your training progresses, expect to become frustrated at regular intervals. This frustration is due to the reaching of plateaus, or short periods of your training wherein you do not progress further until a certain period of experience is achieved. Exactly why these plateaus occur no one really knows, but it is a fact that at times you will not seem to be able to utilize properly new knowledge until you have made do with the old knowledge for a while. These are really periods in which you should be encouraged, for an upswing is just around the corner; however, most people tend to become frustrated. This frustration can be good, if channelled into motivation and determination. It can be bad, however, if allowed to degrade into discouragement.

Discouragement is certainly the greatest enemy of the progressing martial artist. More students of the arts are lost due to discouragement than for any other reason. But a thorough understanding of the cause of discouragement and the proper way to handle it can keep a student training with an "I can" attitude instead of losing to the doldrums of negativism.

Respect for Others and Self

Respect for authority has always been a mandatory virtue for those studying the martial arts. Considerable class time is spent learning techniques which are potentially harmful — both to others and to yourself — if practiced incorrectly, carelessly, or with a poor attitude. The authority within the class — the instructor and the senior students — has the task of controlling this atmosphere and maintaining caution and awareness within the students. Respect for this authority keeps the students working productively and safely. Likewise, respect for one another encourages careful practice and is what keeps our attitudes nonviolent even though we practice a potentially violent art.

Self-respect is certainly the most important virtue any of us could have. With the development of self-discipline and the satisfaction that comes with setting and meeting productive goals, our feelings of self-worth and self-respect are increased. As our respect for ourself grows, respect for others naturally follows. Without self-respect we are defeated before we start. With it, we can never be losers.

Humility

It has been said that "conceit is the quicksand of success," and this is as true in the martial arts as anywhere else. While confidence should be constantly built and strengthened, the ego must be controlled. If not, you will see whatever success you have built slipping from you as in quicksand. If we let it slip far enough, it could be irretrievable.

The temptation of ego usually is strongest following a period of intense confidence-building, such as the new student who rapidly progresses through his or her first few belt ranks, or the green belt who has suddenly won several tournaments in a row. It's fine to talk about such successes as long as such talk really concerns hope for future success. However, boasting about the past, when we have neither set new goals nor formulated a plan for reaching them, is usually our ego desperately attempting to shore up unstable confidence. The approval of others for deeds already done is only a temporary confidence booster, and has the added side effect of often creating an image of ourselves in the eyes of others that we may not really be able to live up to. A much better plan is to constantly set new goals as we attain old ones. Let our progress speak for itself, rather than have us speak for it. Those really interested will know the goals we have reached and respect us for it.

Even more important than *appearing* humble and unconceited is to actually be humble and unconceited. Spending our time thinking about past success only distracts our attention from new tasks at hand. We must constantly avoid the trap of reliving past deeds, and must accept success and satisfaction while looking ahead. New challenges are our goals, new goals that will help us progress further as a martial artist and as a person.

Chapter 5
Conditioning for Karate

STAMINA

Stamina, or endurance, is very important to every martial artist. A lack of endurance will seriously limit the length of time for your karate workouts and the intensity with which you can practice, resulting in short, slow-paced, relatively unproductive training sessions. Should you need to exhibit your skill for any length of time for an important reason, such as a ranking test, a competition match, or an actual confrontation, you may find yourself fading out when it counts most. Also, a body with endurance is generally a healthy body, with efficiently operating muscles, adequate blood supply, a strong heart, and an overall well-developed oxygen-processing system. Good stamina is usually an indication of good general health and conditioning — primary goals of any martial arts system.

Stamina, or general endurance, usually refers to the ability of the body to function under a workload for a period of time. Stamina does not refer to strength of particular body parts, but rather the ability of the respiratory and circulatory systems to provide body parts with the oxygen necessary to maintain function under a particular amount of stress. (This stress could be punching, kicking, running, swimming, or anything else that makes you physically tired.) Your respiratory and circulatory systems may have atrophied through a lack of sustained use or by contact with regular contaminants such as tobacco smoke or city smog.

Fortunately, in an otherwise healthy individual, this lack of endurance is easily reversible, and your ability to process oxygen efficiently may be increased many-fold. Your lungs can be conditioned to process oxygen in your body faster and in larger quantities, your blood supply can be increased and new blood vessels opened, and your heart can be developed into a stronger and more efficient blood pump.

Building stamina is easy to describe and difficult to do. Any exercise that raises the heart rate to its prescribed target zone and keeps it there for 20-30 minutes will result in building stamina. Such exercise may be running, swimming, punching, kicking, sparring, running forms, or any other activity performed with reasonable intensity. Stamina is difficult to achieve, however, because the key ingredients, as in flexibility training, are *consistency* and *patience.* Stamina training must be carried out on a regular schedule and continued long enough to show results. Many trainees have ended their stamina work too soon because the enthusiasm of the first week was replaced in the second week by soreness and no apparent results. The important thing to remember is to hang in there! The muscle soreness will gradually diminish and you will achieve endurance if you stick with your schedule. If you feel as though you're becoming weaker, take a day off to give your body extra time for rebuilding. You should then move back on schedule; it only takes a few days of inactivity to begin losing the strength endurance you worked so hard to gain.

In the early stages of karate training, your in-class activity will undoubtedly build stamina. However, as time goes by and you acquire more endurance, you will find your karate workouts don't tire you as much as they once did. A supplemental program of running, swimming, or cycling added at this point will continue the endurance-building process. Take care, however, to schedule the stamina-building activity *after* your karate workout, or at least several hours *before,* to prevent fatigue from interfering with your karate performance. Table 5-2 shows a week-by-week endurance-building plan.

STRENGTH

Strength-training can be very beneficial to a martial artist. Generally speaking, stronger muscles will produce more endurance and faster techniques. Since this means greater acceleration of an arm or leg, your strikes will theoretically hit with more force (since physics defines force as the mass of an object times its acceleration). A stronger muscle also means less potential energy needed to expend for each job performed and thus more muscular endurance.

Table 5-1 lists each muscle group you will want to strengthen, the appropriate exercises for building each group, and the specific karate technique requiring extensive use of that muscle group. Refer to the Appendix for an illustration of body muscles.

To get the most from your strength workouts, take time to learn the proper way to perform each exercise. Your instructor will be familiar with the calisthenics, while machine and free weight facilities usually have instructors who can familiarize you with their equipment.

Following are additional hints which should add efficiency and results to your strength workouts.

Conditioning

Assisted sit ups

Assisted side ups

Assisted push ups

Assisted calf raise

1. Concentrate on *building* strength, rather than *demonstrating* strength. How much weight you can move should not be a concern, unless you plan to enter a power-lifting contest. Pick an amount of weight for each exercise that will enable you to do the correct number of repetitions (8-12) in the proper manner.

2. All exercises should be performed to the point of *muscular failure* (the point at which another repetition cannot be properly performed). Exercise duration should be limited to one set of 8-12 repetitions, unless otherwise directed by an instructor.

3. Try to use a partner when training without weights. Having this partner add resistance to your exercises will allow you to reduce the number of repetitions required to fatigue your muscles, and therefore perform a more efficient exercise. Have your partner add enough resistance to cause muscular failure at about 8-12 repetitions. (See the illustrations above for some suggested partner exercises.)

4. Never hold your breath while performing repetitions. Breath-holding causes blood pressure to rise and can be dangerous. Instead, breathe in a normal fashion, timing your exhalations to coincide with your muscular exertions.

5. Don't overtrain. A workout involving 8-12 exercises worked to muscular failure three times a week (but never on consecutive days) comprises the "standard" workout. There are many useful variations to this, however, and a qualified weight training instructor or manual can advise you on whether a modified program would better suit your needs.

6. For safety reasons, always warm up slightly before weight training. You may jump rope, lift a light weight, cycle — anything that will help you break a light sweat, indicating rising body temperature. (You want your muscles warm and pliable before placing stress on them.) Also, never lift weights while alone, no matter what equipment you are using, and always use an amount of weight you can control.

DIET

The recommended diet for martial artists is no different from that recommended for other athletes. Adequate amounts of calories, water, and nutrients must be consumed in order to maintain maximum physical performance and facilitate increases in strength and conditioning. Unfortunately, this recommended diet varies depending on who you talk to. Many "experts" on nutrition vary greatly in their dietary beliefs, with some bordering on fanaticism. Many athletes claim to have found a "secret" diet that provides for superhuman performance.

While talk of vegetarian diets, raw-egg milk shakes, and bee pollen may make interesting conversation, be assured there is no magical diet which will instantly bring you that supercharged performance worthy of a champion athlete. All you can do is provide your body with the fuel and building blocks it needs. The rest comes from plain hard work.

Although knowledge of nutrition, like any other science, is still far from complete, we do have a good basic understanding of the interrelationship between food and nutrient consumption and physical performance. For purposes of a brief overview, the foods we consume can be divided into basic food groups (proteins, carbohydrates, and fats), micronutrients (vitamins and minerals), and water.

Proteins

Protein is the basic substance of all tissue structure. Proteins are really combinations of smaller units known as **amino acids.** Which amino acids are present, and in what combination and quantity, determine the type of protein. When you eat protein, your body breaks that protein's structure down into its various constituent amino acids. After absorption of these amino acids through the intestines, your body reassembles these amino acids into the particular kind of protein structures required. Some amino acids may go to repair a skin abrasion, overstretched ligament, or liver damage caused by alcohol consumed last night; others may be added to your chest muscles to increase their size in response to the bench presses you performed yesterday; and still other amino acids may be turned into fuel to be used for energy (although this process is less efficient than simply using carbohydrates for energy, and is thus performed less often.)

As an active athlete you need approximately one gram of protein per kilogram of body weight (one kilogram equals 2.2 pounds). Some amino acids are more valuable to the body than others, and the proteins that contain these amino acids are known as high-quality proteins. Milk, meat, fish, poultry, and eggs are animal products that contain this high-quality protein. Non-animal sources of high-quality protein include soybeans, lentils, and nuts. Most other non-animal sources, such as bread, cereals, and fruits, contain protein of lesser quality, but these proteins are still valuable to the function of your body.

There is little truth in the popular idea that those athletes wishing to increase strength should eat extra protein. A diet providing 55 to 65 grams of protein daily, including some high-quality protein from animal sources, is adequate for a normal, healthy adult athlete. Eating substantially more than this can actually be harmful to the body's excretory system, particularly the kidneys, and the increase in total calorie consumption can contribute to unwanted extra weight.

Carbohydrates

Carbohydrates are the body's primary source of energy. **Starches,** or **complex sugars,** are the form of carbohydrates found in such foods as breads, corn, rice, pasta, potatoes, and other grains and vegetables. Fruits, honey, and refined sweets contain **simple sugars.** Both forms of carhohydrates are used for energy, although complex sugars take longer to enter the bloodstream due to the need for digestion and breakdown to the simple sugar form. Simple sugar products such as table sugar, candy, and honey, enter the bloodstream faster but may have a dehydrating effect on the body and may upset the insulin balance in the blood. For these reasons, starches are better eaten before workouts, as long as a two to three hour digestion period is allowed before hard exercise.

Cellulose is another form of carbohydrate found in fruits, vegetables, and grain. Cellulose is not digested for energy in humans in the same manner as starches, but performs an important function by providing *bulk* and *fiber* in the diet, important factors in maintaining a healthy excretory system.

A healthy adult athlete should get about 55-60% of his or her needed daily calorie total from carbohydrates. In males this averages about 350 grams of carbohydrate daily; in females this figure is about 275 grams.)

Fats

Fats are needed in the body for energy use (they should provide 20% to 30% of your body's daily caloric needs), and because they often carry the fat-soluble vitamins A, D, E, and K. Fats are broken down into **fatty acids** by your body, and these fatty acids are then used for energy or for production of certain body fluids and oils.

Fats contain more than twice as much energy per unit of weight than carbohydrates, but are used for energy within the body in a much less efficient manner than carbohydrates. They are, therefore, better suited for storage as an energy source rather than immediate use, and this is exactly what happens when you eat more fat than your body can immediately use. In men, this excess fat is stored mainly around the midsection and back; in women, the arms and upper legs/buttocks are primary storage areas.

Martial artists should maintain an amount of body fat that leaves them neither too lean nor too fatty. Some fat storage is needed to provide protection and insulation for the body and organs, as well as energy storage, but too much body fat places an increased load on the muscular, respiratory, and circulatory systems of the body. Fatigue sets in sooner during exercise, the body's ability to regulate its temperature is impaired, and the extra weight causes the martial artist to lose speed in movements. Desirable weights for men and women in their early twenties are presented in Table 5-3.

Common sources of fats are meats, eggs, milk, cooking or salad oils, mayonnaise, butter, cheese, nuts, cream, chocolate, avocados, olives, soybeans, and some fish such as salmon and sardines.

Water

Water can be considered as an essential dietary item, although the need for water is much more pronounced and frequent than that for food or nutrients. At one time, water was seen as something to be "denied" to athletes during training. Coaches and trainers in all kinds of sports felt that if they prevented their athletes from consuming water during workouts, they could somehow "train" their bodies to do without water for long periods of time. We know now that this is a false notion and one that can be extremely dangerous. Not only does an athlete's performance suffer when water is withheld, but the risk of heat exhaustion or potentially fatal heat stroke increases dramatically once the body becomes dehydrated during exercise.

Water enables food to be digested and processed for energy, and also regulates body temperature. Its presence for energy production is so crucial that an athlete's performance begins to decrease even before he or she feels a great need for liquids. For this reason, karate workouts, as well as any type of physical activity, should be interrupted regularly to consume a small to moderate amount of water or other non-sugary liquid mixture.

Micronutrients

Micronutrients are the vitamins and minerals necessary for the biologic functions our bodies must fulfill, including those functions providing energy for exercising. The vitamins and minerals the martial artist should be concerned with obtaining are listed in Table 5-4. Whether or not dietary supplements should be purchased and consumed depends upon the quality of the diet. Vitamin deficiencies are virtually unknown in America. Mineral deficiencies of a nonacute nature are seen more frequently, however, particularly deficiencies of the electrolytes **calcium** and **potassium** (causing muscle cramps), and iron among menstruating women (causing anemia).

FLEXIBILITY

One of the most important areas of conditioning for karate is the development of flexibility. The physical height to which you will eventually be able to kick, and ease with which you will execute your lower kicks, will be determined to a great extent by the flexibility which you produce within yourself.

Notice the word "produce," because that is exactly what happens in most cases. Very few flexible martial artists started out that way — most got there through hard work and perserverance.

While development of flexibility is important, don't let it occupy a position in your mind that it doesn't deserve. A nonflexible martial artist, well-versed in the other areas of the art, is much better off than one who boasts great flexibility but has few real martial skills.

Chapter 6 will detail the important principles, stretches, and helpful hints that will enable you to achieve your maximum flexibility potential.

TABLE 5-1

(See the Appendix for the location of each muscle group.)

Muscle Groups	Free Weights	Nautilus Machine	Calisthenics	Karate Application
Calves	calf raise	calf raise on multi-exercise	calf raise	front kick and ankle stability
Hamstrings	squat	leg curl and leg press; squat machine	side and back kicks holds	back and hook kicks
Quadriceps	squat	leg extension; leg press; squat machine	front kick holds	all kicks
Abductors	squat	abductor machine	side and round kick holds	side, hook and roundhouse kicks, outside crescent kicks
Adductors	squat	adductor machine	leg raise	inside crescent kicks
Hip Flexors		leg raise on multi-exerciser or leg curl machine	leg raise	all front and crescent kicks
Abdominals	sit-ups with barbells	abdominal machine	sit-ups	blow absorption and abdominal power in all techniques
Lower Back and Buttocks	squat	hip and back, squat and leg press machine	side and back kick holds	side, back and hook kicks
Obliques	side bend with barbell	rotary oblique machine	side-ups	all kicks, twisting power in punches
Latissimus Dorsi	bent-over rowing, bent and stiff-armed pullover	pullover, behind neck, torso/arm machines; chin-ups on multi-exerciser	chin-ups, parallel pull-ups	pulling-in motions and rear elbow strikes, all downward strikes
Pectorals	bench press, dumbbell flies	fly and decline press machine; parallel dips on multi-exerciser	dips, push-ups	all front punching and striking motions
Deltoids	front and side raises, overhead press	lateral raise, overhead press, rowing torso machines	push-ups	rising blocks and strikes to front and side; parallel strikes to side

Trapezius	shoulder shrug	neck and shoulder shrug machine, rowing torso machine	pulling motions and upward hand strikes
Biceps	standing curl	compound curl and biceps curl machines, chin-ups on multi-exerciser	grabbing, hooking punches and hand strikes
Triceps	triceps extensors	compound and tricep extensor machines, parallel dip on multi-extensor	push-ups, dips	all front punching and striking motions, upper and lower forearm blocks
Forearms	wrist curl	wrist curl on multi-exercise	grabbing motions and wrist stability
Neck	neck curls	4-way neck machines, rotary neck machines, and shoulder shrug machine	blow absorption and attacks using the head as a weapon

TABLE 5-2
RUNNING EXERCISE PROGRAM*
(under 30 years of age)

WEEK	DISTANCE (miles)	Time GOAL (MIN)	FREQ/WK
1	2.0	32:00	3
2	2.0	30:30	3
3	2.0	27:00	3
4	2.0	26:00	3
5	2.0	25:00	3
6	2.0	24:30	3
7	2.0	24:00	3
8	2.0	22:00	3
9	2.0	21:00	3
10	2.0	19:00	3
11	2.0	18:00	4
12	2.0 or 2.5	<17:00 <22:00	4 3

*Start the program by walking, then walk and run, or run, as necessary to meet the changing time goals. (From Cooper, K.H. *The Aerobics Way* (New York: Bantam Books), 1977.

TABLE 5-3

DESIRABLE WEIGHTS FOR WOMEN

Weights listed without clothing according to height without shoes. (From U.S. Department of Agriculture, *Food and Your Weight,* Washington, D.C.: U.S. Government Printing Office, 1973)

Height (feet, inches)	Below Average	Weight (lbs.) Average	Above Average
5 - 0	100	109	118
5 - 1	104	112	121
5 - 2	107	115	125
5 - 3	110	118	128
5 - 4	113	122	132
5 - 5	116	125	135
5 - 6	120	129	139
5 - 7	123	132	142
5 - 8	126	136	146
5 - 9	130	140	151
5 - 10	133	144	156
5 - 11	137	148	161
6 - 0	141	152	166

DESIRABLE WEIGHTS FOR MEN

Weights listed without clothing according to height without shoes. (From U.S. Department of Agriculture, *Food and Your Weight,* Washington, D.C.: U.S. Government Printing Office, 1973)

Height (feet, inches)	Below Average	Weight (lbs.) Average	Above Average
5 - 3	118	129	141
5 - 4	122	133	145
5 - 5	126	137	149
5 - 6	130	142	155
5 - 7	134	147	161
5 - 8	139	151	166
5 - 9	143	155	170
5 - 10	147	159	174
5 - 11	150	163	178
6 - 0	154	167	183
6 - 1	158	171	188
6 - 2	162	175	192
6 - 3	165	178	195

TABLE 5-4
Essential Vitamins for the Martial Artist

VITAMIN	RDA males 19-22 yrs.	RDA females 19-22 yrs.	Use in body	Common Sources
A (Retinol)	5,000 IU	4,000 IU	vision, cell membrane structure	dark green, deep yellow or red vegetables, liver, eggs
B_1 (Thiamin)	1.5 mg.	1.1 mg.	carbohydrate metabolism	meats, green leafy vegetables, cereals, nuts, berries, legumes
B_2 (Riboflavin)	1.8 mg.	1.4 mg.	catalyst for certain cellular oxidations	meats, dairy products, green leafy vegetables cereals, eggs, legumes
Niacin	20 mg.	14 mg.	constituent of certain important coenzymes	meats, fish, cereals, peas and beans, nuts
B_6 (Pyridoxine)	2.0 mg.	2.0 mg.	coenzymes for amino acid metabolism	meats, cereals, nuts, soybeans, corn, most vegetables
B_{12} (Cyanocobalamine)	3.0 mg.	3.0 mg.	nucleic acid and nucleo-protein synthesis	meats, dairy products, fish, human intestinal flora
Biotin	300 mg.	300 mg.	coenzyme for carbohydrate metabolism	milk, intestinal flora, liver, eggs, peanuts, beans, mushrooms

Folacin (Folic Acid)	400 mg.	nucleic acid synthesis, red blood cell synthesis	liver, green leafy vegetables, nuts, cereals, lentils
Pantothenic Acid	10 mg.	coenzyme for carbohydrate, fat and protein metabolism	organ meats, eggs, nuts, flowery and leafy vegetables, grains
C (Ascorbic Acid)	45 mg.	amino acid metabolism, connective tissue formation	citrus fruits, flowery and leafy vegetables, tomatoes, potatoes
D (Calciferol)	400 IU	facilitates use of calcium and phosphorus	sunlight, milk, eggs, liver, enriched dairy products
E (Tocopherol)	15 IU	antioxidant for certain essential compounds	wheat, soybean, corn and cottonseed germ oils, eggs and meats
K (Menadione)	none set probably 50-100 mg.	required for synthesis of blood clotting factors	human intestinal flora, green leafy vegetables, liver

CHAPTER 5 EVALUATION

Multiple Choice: Circle the letter of the correct answer.
1. Stamina-building workouts are best carried out
   a. immediately *before* karate class.
   b. immediately *before* or *after* karate class.
   c. several hours *before* karate class, or during class breaks.
   d. several hours *before* karate class, or after class.
2. All strength-building exercises should be continued to the point of
   a. muscular failure.
   b. moderate muscle fatigue.
   c. a pre-arranged number of repetitions, regardless of the fatigue point.
   d. unconciousness.
3. The recommended diet for martial artists
   a. differs from that of other athletes in that increased protein and carbohydrates are needed.
   b. does not differ from that of other athletes, since all athletic diets require excess protein amounts.
   c. does not differ from that of other athletes, since all athletics require adequate amounts of calories, water, and nutrients.
4. Karate workouts should be interrupted for water breaks
   a. as soon as everyone starts feeling thristy.
   b. regularly, whether everyone feels a great thirst or not.
   c. as soon as signs of heat stroke become apparent among the students.
   d. never, since the body must be trained to operate without water for long periods.
5. The type of carbohydrate most suitable for eating before workouts is
   a. cellulose
   b. complex sugars
   c. honey
   d. simple sugars

Fill in the blanks:
1. Stamina generally refers to the ability of the respiratory and circulatory systems to provide other body parts with _____ while under stress.

2. Generally speaking, stronger muscles produce _____ techniques, resulting in strikes landing with greater _____.

3. The quadricep muscles are used during all _____ techniques.

4. When strength-training, concentrate on _____ strength, rather than _____ strength.

5. Exercises performed to muscular failure should consist of _____ set of _____ repetitions.

Questions for Thought and Essay:
Why should exercises such as running, swimming, or cycling be utilized for stamina work, rather than simply repeating karate techniques over and over until the training effect is achieved?

Chapter 6
Developing Flexibility

BASIC PRINCIPLES

The underlying principle of exercise is to allow a muscle or joint to become flexible, rather than trying to force it. Slowly stretching the muscle or joint to its limits, combined with a hold of eight seconds or more, will eventually produce a muscle accustomed to elongation and a joint with an increased range of motion. On the other hand, forcing a muscle or joint against pain will only result in a torn muscle or ligament, requiring time off for healing, and scar tissue which will tend to inhibit future flexibility development.

Consistency and patience are also primary to the development of flexibility. Stretching exercises should be performed at least once a day, although high intensity, "go a little further than last time," stretching sessions should be performed no more than four times per week, and spaced with days in which you do only enough to "stay loose." Developing flexibility takes time. This does not mean days or weeks. While improvement will be seen within six months, years will be required to really maximize your potential. Nearly anyone can become flexible enough to execute all basic karate techniques and a select few "genetically — gifted" students can, with consistent work, reach the levels of flexibility generally associated with advanced gymnasts and dancers.

As you begin your practice of the following exercises, remember always to *warm up* before starting to practice, particularly in cold weather. A little rope-jumping or a short jog will make quite a difference in the starting point of your stretch at any given workout. Also, try to *relax* the muscle you're stretching. If it's tense, it won't stretch. Relax it, and hold it at the point at which you feel it stretching. If it really begins to *hurt,* ease up! It's your body's way of saying "too far too soon." Just follow correct technique, be patient, and you'll achieve the results you want.

Before beginning the following exercises, familiarize yourself with the muscles you will be stretching by referring to Appendix G.

STRETCHING EXERCISES

The following exercises demonstrate both solitary and partner-assisted common stretches. In all cases, the back should be kept straight and the muscle to be stretched should be relaxed. When working with a partner, be certain the partner applies pressure only in small, graduated amounts, and always to the lower back rather than near the shoulders or neck. Also, tensing the muscle to be stretched just before relaxing it tends to produce an even greater state of relaxation, and is a desirable practice.

Neck Circles: Slowly bend your head to each side and to the front and rear. Hold for several seconds in each direction before relaxing. This exercise prevents injuries due to sudden head movements.

Side Bends: Grasp your hands overhead and bend to one side. This stretch will include the back of your shoulder, latissimus muscles, and obliques.

LOWER BODY
Seated Hamstring Stretch: The leg not being stretched is bent inward. The objective is to bend low at the waist, bringing the chest close to the knee. Keep looking at your toes, which are also pointed up. Relax the hamstring muscles on the leg being stretched. A partner may assist by pushing gently on the lower back.

Calf Stretch: With both feet in front and legs together, grasp the soles of your feet and pull your heels off the floor. Hold for 5 seconds, then relax slowly. Keep your calves relaxed throughout.

Hamstring/Lower Back Stretch: With both feet together and toes up, slowly bend chest to knees and hold. Keep head up, knees straight, and bend *low* at the waist. Keep hamstrings and lower back relaxed. A partner may assist by pushing gently on the lower back.

Thigh/Lower Back Stretch: From a kneeling position, lean back with your weight on your elbows until you feel the stretch in your thighs and lower back. Do not involve your head or neck in the stretch.

Twisting Hip Stretch: The left foot is placed on the outside of the knee of the right leg. The right elbow is placed on the left side of the left knee. Using the left hand on the ground for support, twist to your left, and push your knee toward the right with your right elbow. You'll feel the stretch in your left hip. Repeat to the other side.

Butterfly Groin Stretches: With your knees bent and soles of your feet together, grasp your feet and push your knees toward the ground with your elbows. Relax the inner thigh and hip muscles being stretched.

Front Bends from Butterfly Position: Keeping your legs relaxed and your back straight, pull yourself down to the front. Keep your head up and try to touch your chest to your feet. A partner may assist by pushing gently on the lower back.

Hamstring Inner Thigh Stretch: With legs wide apart and toes up, bend slowly to each side. Work your chest toward the outside of the knee, then the inside. The further toward the inside of the knee you move, the more you will involve the inner thigh or *adductor* muscles. You will also notice this stretch helps loosen up the side, or *oblique,* muscles. A partner may assist by pushing gently on the lower back.

Inner Thigh Stretch: With legs apart and toes up, bend directly to the front. Keep your head up and work your chest toward the ground. The back must remain straight and the bend should be from the lower waist. A partner may assist by pushing gently on the lower back.

Developing Flexibility 65

Knee Splits: This stretch works the inner thigh area without involving the hamstrings or placing undue strain on the inner knee. You must relax and slowly work your knees to the outside. A partner may assist by applying gentle downward pressure on the extreme low back area.

Hurdler Stretch: The leg to be stretched should be extended with the toes up and the rear leg bent with the knee pointed as far backward as possible. Bend low at the waist and try to bring your chest to your knee, keeping your head up. This stretch works both the hamstring of the extended leg and the groin area, and may be partner-assisted in the same manner as the other hamstring stretches. Caution should be exercised, however, that this stretch is not taken to such an extreme as to cause pain in the knee of the rear leg.

Full Side Split: Keeping your weight on your hands, move your feet to the outside until you feel the stretch in your inner thighs. "Walking" your hands to the front will bring the stretch more around the the front of the hips, while "walking" to the rear will incorporate more hamstring stretch.

Half Front Split: Attempt to move your feet into a progressively longer stance, stretching the upper hamstring area of the forward leg and the frontal thigh (quadriceps) of the rear leg.

Full Front Split: From the half front split position, ease yourself down into a full split, keeping your weight on your hands and avoiding undue stress to the rear knee. The stretch will be in the hamstring of the front leg, the quadriceps of the rear leg, and the entire hip area.

Squatting Hamstring/Groin Stretch: From a standing position with the feet shoulder-width apart, squat over your right foot, keeping that foot flat on the floor, and extend the left leg, keeping the toes pointing upwards. Support your weight on your left hand which is placed behind you, and use your right hand to push your right knee to the outside. You should feel the stretch in your left hamstring and groin area. To advance this stretch, the feet may be moved farther apart, and the supporting hand may be placed on the ankle of the extended leg, requiring a forward body lean and bringing more of a stretch to the hamstring. Repeat to the opposite side.

Assisted Wall Stretch — Front: With your back to the wall and your supporting foot turned to the outside, have your partner slowly raise your leg to the front, stretching the hamstring of that leg. Hold, relax, and repeat.

Assisted Wall Stretch — Side: Turn your supporting foot to the wall and have your partner raise your leg to the side. Keep your hips rolled to the front and arch your back slightly. You will feel this stretch on the adductor muscles, and the hamstring of the supporting leg.

Hints for Maximum Progress and Avoiding Injury

1. Tensing the muscle to be stretched for several seconds before beginning your stretch will bring about a greater degree of relaxation within that muscle. Allowing a muscle to tense up *during* a stretch will lead only to reduced progress and possible injury.

2. Always stretch *slowly.* Never bounce or force a stretch. Slowly take the muscle to the point where you feel it stretching and hold it for a minimum of six seconds. After your body becomes more limber and accustomed to stretching, you will actually be able to feel the muscle elongating itself as you stretch out prior to a workout.

3. Pain, when stretching, does not mean more gain! Take a stretch only to the point of muscle resistance, and hold the stretch against that resistance. This may be uncomfortable but should never be so painful that it is an ordeal to maintain the stretch. In particular, a burning sensation is usually an indication of a muscle in the process of being overstretched, or "pulled." Pulled muscles are not only painful and delay your return to action, but may also produce scar tissue which can permanently limit the stretching potential of that muscle.

4. Always warm up before beginning your stretching routine. Jump rope, jog, or do anything to cause a light sweat and increased body temperature. The circulation increase within your muscles and connective tissue will enable your muscles to stretch further with less likelihood of injury.

5. Never "snap back" to a resting position from a stretch. Slowly relax the pressure on the joint or muscle, allowing your body to return to the unstretched position gradually.

6. When using a partner to help you stretch, make certain the partner applies pressure slowly and stops when you ask. If it is a "bent over" type stretch, make sure the partner pushes *low* on your back, near the waist, to avoid back injuries. When doing this type of stretch alone, follow these same guidelines. Remember, the object is not to touch your head to your knee, but to gain a safe, productive stretch in the muscle being worked.

7. Some stretches may place some stress on the knee joint. Be careful not to injure this important but relatively weak joint by pushing your stretch too far too soon. There's a good chance you could pull a knee ligament before pulling a muscle.

8. Should you injure a muscle, you will feel a sudden, burning pain that continues to throb even after the stretching pressure is removed. *Do not continue to stretch the muscle.* Rather, cease work and immediately apply ice to the injured area. Despit the temptation to "do something to make it better," leave it alone for a day or so. Aspirin, if recommended by a physician, usually alleviates the pain.

Heat, in the form of warm water, should be applied no sooner than 48 hours after the injury occurs, and then only as a means of increasing circulation to the area. Stretching should be very light and begin no sooner than 72 hours after the injury. If sharp pain is encountered even with this light stretch, discontinue immediately and wait another day before trying again. If the pull seems no better after 96 hours, consider seeing your physician or physical therapist for professional advice on the injury.

9. As a final word on stretching, remember that nothing worth having comes without a price, and flexibility is no exception. In this case the price is *time, self-discipline,* and *patience.* You must make the time to stretch, stretch the proper way, and understand that results will not come overnight. Also, you must do all the stretches, not just the ones you like to do or can do well. Work hard, and keep a positive attitude.

CHAPTER 6 EVALUATION

Multiple Choice: Circle the letter of the correct answer.
1. Bouncing while stretching can lead to:
   a. increased flexibility achieved within a shorter than normal time period.
   b. increased flexibility, but within a longer than normal time period
   c. possible loss of endurance and tone within the muscle being stretched, due to rapid elongation
   d. torn muscles and ligaments, and possible scar tissue development
2. Stretching exercises should be performed:
   a. Once a day only
   b. at least once a day
   c. never more than three times per day
   d. twice a day, morning and afternoon
3. "Side bends" are designed to stretch:
   a. chest muscles, obliques, and hamstrings
   b. obliques, back of shoulders, and latissimus muscles
   c. obliques, back of shoulders, and hamstrings
   d. quadriceps, obliques, and latissimus muscles
4. To allow for greater stretching potential, a muscle should be tensed:
   a. just before stretching
   b. during stretching
   c. just after stretching
   d. tensing a muscle can never help stretch it
5. Upon feeling the symptoms of a "pulled" muscle, you should immediately:
   a. cease stretching and apply heat to the injured area
   b. cease stretching and apply ice to the injured area
   c. continue stretching, and try to "work out" the injury
   d. see an orthopedic specialist immediately

Fill in the blanks:
1. Although dramatic increases in flexibility are seen within _____, it will take _____ before most students realize their maximum flexibility potential.

2. The physiological idea of stretching is to produce muscles accustomed to repeated _____, and joints with increased _____ of _____.

3. During all stretching exercises, the back should be kept _____ and any pressure applied by an assistant should be to the _____ area of the back only.

4. "Butterfly" stretches work the _____ and inner _____ areas. "Knee splits" work the inner _____ area without involving the _____ muscles or placing a strain on the _____.

5. The knee joint is relatively easy to injure during stretching by applying too much pressure too soon during certain stretches, or by applying improper form. Caution should be exercised particularly during the _____, _____, _____, _____, _____ stretches, as these exercises place increased stress on the knee joint.

Questions for Thought and Essay:
Considerable class time is spent on flexibility development. Why do you think flexibility is important to you as a martial artist? What is its importance relative to the other areas of physical development within karate?

Chapter 7
Stances

Karate techniques are only as effective as the stance from which they are executed. The importance of the stance cannot be overemphasized. Even flying kicks, which strike the target while the kicker is airborne, must begin with a solid take-off stance. Without a strong, properly balanced stance, any fighter's technique will lack the foundation necessary for effective deployment of kicks, punches and blocks.

Basic physics states that when one object strikes another, an equal force is generated in both directions. This means that when you punch or kick a target, at the moment of impact the target is really pushing against your hand or foot with a force equal to that with which you strike it. If your technique is executed properly and your stance is firm, the target will absorb the shock. If your stance is not firm and solid with proper body positioning and weight distribution, *you*, rather than the target, will absorb the force of the strike.

Different stances are used to execute different techniques. Some stances are suitable for many techniques and fighting situations while others are more specialized. Similarly, some techniques can be executed from any stances, while others are suitable for execution from only one or two.

The general types of stances learned in the beginning levels of martial arts training are described in this chapter. Still other stances are learned at the intermediate and advanced levels, but one never abandons the basic stances. Many modifications of these basic stances are widely practiced, depending upon the particular style of karate and the instructor's preferences.

Attention stance.

Bowing from attention stance.

Ready stance.

ATTENTION STANCE

The attention stance is used by many styles during training and at the beginning of forms as a stance from which to bow as a sign of respect and good intentions. The feet are pointed out at a 45-degree angle and the arms are at the sides with the hands open. (In some styles the arms are to the front and the fists closed.) The bow is executed by simply bending forward 45 degrees from the waist, keeping the eyes up.

READY STANCE

The ready position is used during training as a transition stance between the attention stance and fighting stance. Occasionally techniques may be executed from this stance, usually during forms. The feet are apart (the length of one foot) and pointed straight ahead; the hands are in fists at the sides.

SIDE (STRADDLE) STANCE

Sometimes the side (straddle) stance is referred to as the "horse" or "square-horse" stance. It is used during training as a stance from which to teach basic techniques, and during fighting as a stance from which to execute such side-fighting technique as the backfist or side kick. This stance presents very little of your body as a target to the opponent. The feet are approximately shoulder-width apart and pointed straight ahead. The back is straight and the shoulders square. Weight is equally distributed on both feet.

Side (straddle) stance.    *Front stance.*    *Back stance.*

FRONT STANCE

The front stance is the basic stance for teaching movement with techniques. It is used more than any other stance during forms, and is used in fighting whenever one's body must face the target, such as during execution of back-leg kicks or front hand/back hand combinations. The feet are not one behind the other, but rather have about a foot's width between them. The length of the stance should be approximately the same as the length of your lower leg. Weight distribution is equal on both feet. The front foot points straight ahead, while the back foot is turned out 45 degrees. The front knee is bent into a 90 degree angle, and the rear leg is either straight or bent slightly, depending on the technique being executed. The hips are to the front or turned 20 degrees to the side.

BACK STANCE

A stance seen quite often in forms, the back stance is not used as much in modern free-fighting. The weight distribution may be 50%-50%, or the rear leg may carry the majority of the body weight, depending on the application. This stance sometimes uses the raised-heel posture on the forward leg to facilitate front-leg kicking and mobility. The back knee and foot are turned to the side, and the hips face 45 degrees off the front line. This stance first appears in forms during the early intermediate stages. The length of this stance is about the same as the width of the side stance.

Chapter 8
Principles of Effective Technique

The martial artist should be aware not only of the skills needed to practice but of the physical law and principles that make the difference between just executing technique, and executing effective technique. An understanding of why some movements are effective and others aren't is an important step toward learning to practice technique in the proper way. The practice of ineffective technique only reinforces bad habits that become increasingly hard to break.

The factors that make techniques physically effective include the following:

1. **Force.** The amount of total impact one object exerts on another upon contact. The object may be your fist and the opponent's face or your foot and the opponent's ribs.

2. **Stability.** The degree of equilibrium and support one maintains. Without stability, the force you exert in your techniques will be not only useless, but can actually work against you.

3. **Accuracy.** The ability to "focus" a strike on a target in a two-dimensional sense (that is, up or down and left to right), and in the three-dimensional concept of depth.

4. **Impact pressure.** The application of total force, with desired effect in mind. The impact pressure will change with the size of the target area.

A detailed look at each of these factors reveals just how important each is to executing techniques that are *effective*.

FORCE

The production of a force to use against an opponent involves speed and mass in an intimate relationship. Specifically, the force produced will be equal to the speed of the striking object multiplied by its mass, or in equation form: $F = ma$ (with F representing *force*, m as *mass*, and a as *acceleration* or the building of speed). Therefore, if we can increase either the speed of an object, or its mass, we can increase the force with which it will strike the target. However, increasing the mass of an object, but *reducing* the speed, will not increase the force. For example, if you hold a weight in your fist that makes your hand and arm twice as heavy but allows you to punch only *half as fast* due to the extra weight, you end up gaining nothing in added force or power. The goal instead is to increase speed, mass, or *both*, without reducing either. An examination of each of these factors reveals how this is accomplished.

Speed

Speed should become a primary goal of the martial artist. Speed not only allows you to land techniques by "beating the block," but actually increases the impact of the strike, as illustrated in the equation $F=ma$. How fast a technique can be executed really means how quickly your hands or feet can be accelerated from a dead stop to high velocity at the moment of impact. One obvious way to do this is to increase the potential energy put into this acceleration by becoming stronger. A larger muscle holds more potential energy which takes a given mass, such as your hand or foot, and accelerates it to a greater velocity in a given distance. The strength-building exercises in Chapter 5 will help to develop this potential.

For maximum speed in technique you should keep all techniques moving in as straight a line to the target as possible, unless a curved motion is an inherent part of the technique. Any change of direction requires energy that could be better used for straight-line speed. Figures 8-1 through 8-3 show a front kick begun with the foot too low. The motion of the kick is therefore an *upward* angle and energy must be used to change the direction of the kick in mid-execution, energy that could be better spent accelerating the kick straight in toward its target.

Figure 8.1

Figure 8.2

Figure 8.3

Another important point to consider is that of *added forces* with regard to speed. To illustrate this, suppose that you are stepping with a straight punch. Attempt to accelerate your body forward into another front stance as quickly as possible (figures 8-4 and 8-5). As your body gains speed moving toward the target, note that your punching hand is also moving forward at an increasing speed, even though you have not yet begun your punch. Therefore, the speed produced while actually throwing the punch (figure 8-6) will be *added to* the speed at which your arm is already moving due to the step. (A similar case occurs when the hip is rotated during the reverse punch.) Greater acceleration and speed (and hence, *force*) are produced at impact (figure 8-7) than could have been produced from either the step or the punch alone. Here again, the value of straight-line motion is evident. Moving from the hips, keeping the center of gravity on a constant horizontal plane (figures 8-4 through 8-7), provides maximum step velocity. Allowing the center of gravity to *rise*

Figure 8.4

Figure 8.5

Figure 8.6

Figure 8.7

78   **Effective Technique**

Figure 8.8

Figure 8.9

Figure 8.10

during the step (figure 8-8 through 8-10), causes the unnecessary use of energy to produce an up and down motion.

Another important factor in achieving maximum speed through muscular contraction is the phenomenon of the "kiai" or "kihap," as it is known in Oriental terms. It is actually a yell emitted upon making contact with a strike or block. An exhalation should always accompany the delivery of a technique, and the "kiai" just adds a loud vocal expression to this exhalation. The effect is very pronounced, however. Forceful exhalations are produced by strong contractions of abdominal and chest muscles, and this helps stabilize the thorax, creating a more powerful technique. In addition, the vocal yell (which takes a variety of audible forms, depending on individual preferences) helps to coordinate all muscular contractions into one simultaneous effect, producing maximum acceleration in all motions.

Mass

Short of the addition of extra weight, mass (the other half of the right side of our force equation) is constant prior to beginning the technique and cannot be altered to increase the total force of a blow. Concentrate instead of gaining maximum utilization of this constant mass, including putting together as many sources of mass as possible into one effect. The secret to doing this is timing. In figures 8-4 through 8-7 the subject executed a straight punch in a step-through fashion. The punch was *timed* to land on the target simultaneously with the completion of the step. This adds the velocities produced by the step and the punch; it also adds the mass (weight) of the body to the mass of the arm, since both are moving forward and stopping at the same time. Thus, the total mass accelerated is greater than with the punch alone, and the striking force is proportionately greater.

Stopping the forward motion of the body before executing the punch, as in figures 8-11 through 8-14, reduces the potential power through increased mass. It also wastes energy, since forward momentum must be stopped by the muscles unless that momentum can be transferred into the target.

Figure 8.11

Figure 8.12

Figure 8.13

Figure 8.14

80 **Effective Technique**

Figure 8.15

Figure 8.16

Another way of accelerating additional mass into a target is through the *rotation* of the body on a pivot. As shown in figures 8-15 and 8-16, the rotation of the hip into the reverse punch not only adds to the speed of the punch, but brings the mass of the rear hip area into forward motion and adds that mass to the total mass being accelerated into the target. Figure 8-17 shows this same hip mass being delivered into a front kick, while figure 8-18 illustrates how upper-body rotation can be added to a jab.

Although the maximum mass that can be utilized for any particular technique is determined prior to execution, the mass of weapons can be changed permanently through proper strength training. Greater muscular size equals greater mass, and all other factors being equal, the more muscular person will hit harder with his or her techniques than the less muscular person. The factors that must be equal, are obviously those that have to do with proper execution of the technique, along with the factors of speed, stability, accuracy, and impact pressure that are covered in this chapter.

Figure 8.17

Figure 8.18

STABILITY

Without stability, your techniques will have no base of support and will be ineffective. Stability must be reduced, obviously, to allow body movement, but should always be maximized upon contact with a strike or block.

Stability is closely related to the center of gravity. In order to maintain enough stability to make your techniques effective, you must understand and apply several basic principles involving your base of support (the area created by the legs in any stance), and your center of gravity.

1. The center of gravity must fall within the boundaries of its base of support. If you lean in your stance far enough in any direction, you will bring your center of gravity outside your base of support, and you will probably find yourself unable to even stay in your stance at all, much less able to execute any techniques. Figure 8-19 shows a jab that has been overextended. The center of gravity has been displaced too far forward, and the subject must now take care not to actually fall forward out of his stance. In figure 8-20 the subject has shifted his center of gravity too far back during blocking, and has actually made himself a prime target for a rear-leg sweep due to lack of stability within the stance.

Figure 8.19

Figure 8.20

2. The greater the area of the base of support, the greater the stability. This statement refers to the **area** (defined as the length times the width) created by the base of support around the center of gravity. In figure 8-21, the subject on the left has assumed a stance that is too short to support his reverse punch. The area created by the base of support (the feet) is not great enough to stabilize the stance. As the reverse punch strikes the target (figure 8-22), the puncher is actually pushed

Figure 8.21

Figure 8.22

Figure 8.23

backward by his own strike, since the opponent's longer stance provides greater stability. The same problem would be true of a reverse punch executed from the stance that is too **narrow,** except the stability problem in that case would be from **side to side.** Figure 8-23 shows the attacker in a stance that is both wide enough and long enough, thereby creating an area large enough to stabilize him as he executes his reverse punch.

3. **The closer the center of gravity to the base of support, the more stability is created.** This explains why the attacker in

Effective Technique

Figure 8-24 is unstable. The height of his center of gravity allows him to take up the shock of his own strike. When he drops lower in his stance (figure 8-25), he creates stability which allows the power of the strike to be transferred to the target. Thus, your stances (and hence, your center of gravity) must remain **low** when executing any strike or block.

Figure 8.24

Figure 8.25

Figure 8.26

Figure 8.27

4. An object is more stable in the direction in which the center of gravity is closest to the edge of the base of support. Therefore, an attacker wishing to execute a side-kick with maximum stability should shift his center of gravity slightly **forward** (figure 8-26), rather than to the rear (figure 8-27). The opposite would be true should the desired movement be to the **rear.** This illustrates the value of "leaning into" the punch or kick.

ACCURACY

In karate, accuracy is a synonymous with focus. **Focus** refers to the placement of a technique at its point of maximum power **in a particular point in space at a particular time.** This three-dimensional concept includes depth as well as height and width. Just as it is important to land a strike on the oponent's chin rather than the cheek or forehead, it is equally as important to land that strike with the desired degree of penetration into the target. The focus can be shallow (figure 8-28), medium (figure 8-29), or deep (figure 8-30).

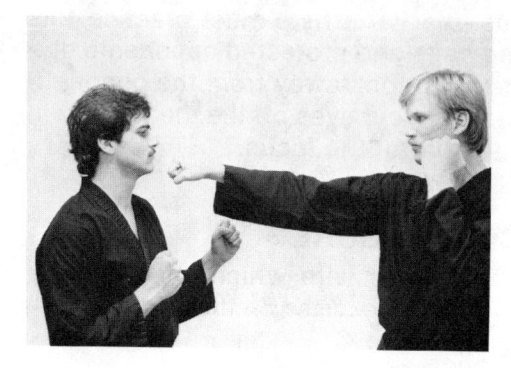

Figure 8.28

Figure 8.29

Figure 8.30

This concept is extremely important, for it ultimately determines the true effect of any techniques executed. This concept enables the martial artist to break boards, bricks, and ice. The martial artist simply focuses on a point an inch or so behind the face of the object to be broken (a deep focus), and does not allow his or her technique to be stopped until that focus point is reached. This concept is also of extreme importance when freesparring and during competitions, since either shallow or medium focus are the maximum allowed during these periods for safety reasons. Deep focus should be reserved for full-contact competitions or actual self-defense situations.

To produce control of focus, martial artists must practice this concept regularly, with striking bags and protected opponents during sparring. It is vital also never to look away from the opponent while executing a technique; taking your eyes off the the target will certainly destroy your ability to control the focus.

IMPACT PRESSURE

The relationship between the **focus** with which one strikes a target and the **pressure** that is actually exerted on the target by that force is seen in the following equation:

$$\text{PRESSURE} = \frac{\text{force}}{\text{area}}$$

Force is that energy exerted against a target by an object's mass times its acceleration into that target; **area** is that physical part of the target that the object is actually making contact with. Therefore, the **pressure** exerted against the target by a strike can be increased by either increasing the force (discussed earlier), or by **decreasing the area over which the force is distributed.**

In karate, there are several ways to capitalize on this force-pressure theory. Striking with only the two large knuckles of the fist concentrates all the punching force into that relatively small area, creating a greater penetrating effect that if all four knuckles were used. Similarly, using the side of the hand on knifehand strikes and the side of the foot on sidekicks increases the effect of these techniques by decreasing the area of contact with the target.

This force-pressure relationship theory allows one to increase further the effect of strikes, even though both the available mass and speed of execution have been maximized already. This is one of the fundamental theories of the martial arts, and explains the devastating effect of karate strikes in comparison to strikes executed by the untrained.

CHAPTER 8 EVALUATION

Multiple Choice: Circle the letter of the correct answer.

1. The **force** produced by any strike will be equal to the **mass** of the striking object multiplied by its
   a. weight
   b. impact pressure
   c. stability factor
   d. acceleration

2. **Straight-line motion,** with either a technique or when moving in our stances, helps maximize
   a. mass
   b. impact pressure
   c. speed
   d. base of support

3. **Stability** within a stance increases with an
   a. increase in the area of the base of support
   b. decrease in the distance between the center of gravity and the edge of the base of support in the direction of the strike
   c. decrease in the distance between the base of support and the center of gravity

4. The **pressure** that is actually exerted on a target by a strike can be calculated by
   a. dividing the **focus** by the **area**
   b. dividing the **force** by the **area**
   c. dividing the **acceleration** by the **area**
   d. multiplying the **mass** times the **acceleration**

5. Therefore, an increase in the pressure exerted by the strike can be accomplished by simply
   a. increasing the force
   b. increasing the area
   c. decreasing the area
   d. a or c

Fill in the blanks:

1. The amount of **force** produced during the execution of a technique can be calculated using an equation that involves the factors of _____ and _____.

2. Two ways to increase the **acceleration** factor of techniques is to be sure our techniques travel _____ and to become _____ ourselves.

3. Timing punches and kicks to land with the completion of forward motion utilizes the principle of _____ to maximize the factors of _____ and _____.

4. The delivery of a technique should always be accompanied by an _____.

5. The term **focus** refers not only to hitting a target in a two-dimensional sense, but also governs the degree of _____ into the target.

Question for Thought and Essay:
If a "kiai" or "kihap" helps to collect and release your potential energy into a strike, and that is a good thing to practice, why not produce this yell on **every** count **every** time you practice?

Chapter 9
Hand Strikes

Punches

To form the karate fist for punches, begin with the hand open, fingers and thumb extended (Fig. 9-1). Curl the fingers inward, touching the fingertips as high as possible on the inner hand (Fig. 9-2). Continue curling the fist inward until the fingernails cannot be seen (figure 9-3). Now tuck the thumb in, bent at the middle joint as far as possible, being sure to touch the middle finger with the tip of the thumb (figure 9-4). The striking surface in all punches is the front of the large knuckles of the index and middle fingers (figure 9-5). The wrist is always held very straight (figure 9-6). (Note: In some styles of Chinese Kung-Fu, particularly the Wing Chun style, the wrist is bent slightly upward on vertical punches and the striking surfaces of the fist are the large knuckles of the ring and little fingers (figure 9-7).

The following strikes comprise the basic punching techniques of most styles of martial arts.

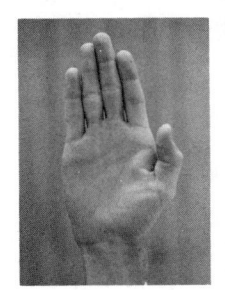

Figure 9.1 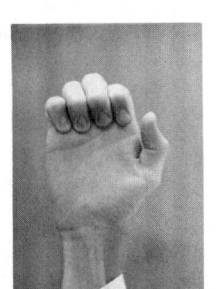　　Figure 9.2 　　Figure 9.3 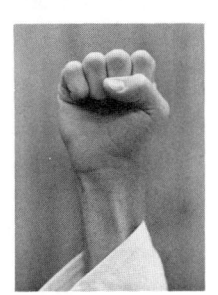　　Figure 9.4

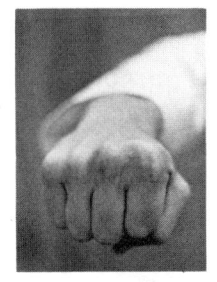

Figure 9.5 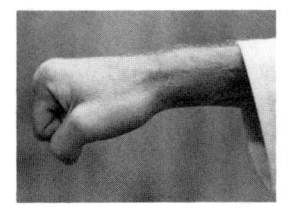　　Figure 9.6 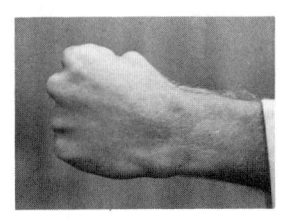　　Figure 9.7

Figure 9.8 　　　　　　Figure 9.9 　　　　　　Figure 9.10

Straight Punch

The straight punch is the basic corkscrew punch executed from an extreme pulled-back position of the fist. The punch is usually executed to the front from a side stance (figure 9-8) with either hand, or from a front stance (figure 9-13) with the front hand. Although seen frequently throughout the forms of most systems, the straight punch, when executed as described, is now known to be undesirable as a true fighting technique. There is very little use of the body for power and the pulled-back position of the hands when preparing to punch affords no protection for the face or body. Other than during forms, this technique is used today primarily as a means of teaching basic punching arm movements to beginning students and familiarizing them with basic action — reaction principles.

As the punching arm begins its extension, the extended arm begins returning to a flexed position. (See figure 9-8 through 9-10). Both fists turn in transit so that at completion, the punching fist is palm **down,** while the "at rest" fist is palm **up** (hence the name "corkscrew punch"). The resting position is high on the rib cage, and is used in most Okinawan and Japanese styles (figure 9-11). Other styles, including most Korean and Chinese styles, use a lower "at rest" fist position, below the bottom rib and close to the hip (figure 9-12). It is very important that the extended arm pulls back to a flexed position **simultaneously** with the extension of the punching arm, not before or after. Figure 9-13 shows the completed punch as executed with the front hand from a front stance.

Jab

The jab is always executed with the front hand from a front or side stance. Although the jab can strike with considerable force when executed properly, it is mainly used as a stunning technique to set the

Hand Strikes 91

Figure 9.11

Figure 9.12

Figure 9.13

opponent up for a stronger finishing blow. A contemporary technique, it is seldom seen in traditional forms, but is an excellent free-fighting technique.

The fighter begins from a front stance with the hands in a basic fighting position. (See figures 9-14 and 9-15.) As the jabbing punch extends, the fist turns and strikes from a horizontal position. The upper body rotates for power and reach, and the weight is shifted to the front leg for the same reasons. The front knee will bend several degrees further as the punch is extended. The bent shoulder is raised slightly and the head dipped so that the chin is covered from the side. The rear hand raises to cover the other side of the face, with the elbow held close to the body for protection from counterstrikes. (These changes in position and weight shifts should occur *simultaneously* with the actual landing of the punch.)

After the jab is completed, the weight shifts back to a normal 50-50 distribution, and the hands return to a standard fighting position (figure 9-16). When used in actual free-fighting, the jab is usually executed simultaneously with a "step-through" or "step-out" delivery method, both to add power and to close the distance to the opponent (see Chapter 14 on delivery methods).

Figure 9.14

Figure 9.15

Figure 9.16

Reverse Punch

Having long been a staple tournament fighters, the reverse punch continues to be one of the favorite techniques of most competitors, self-defense specialists, and traditional karate teachers. It is fast, hard-hitting, and versatile enough to fit well into many action situations, whether on the street or in the tournament ring.

The power in the reverse punch comes from the extreme twisting of the hip timed with the striking of the punch and is used strategically during fighting as a "finishing" blow to the face or body, usually after a set-up using the front hand or a kicking technique.

The primary drawbacks to the reverse punch are the exposure of the frontal part of the body upon completion of the technique (figure 9-19), and the inability to effectively execute it from any stance other than the front stance, since the feet must have considerable depth and width between them to support the hip rotation.

The fighter begins from a front stance with the hands in a basic fighting position (figure 9-17). The back hand travels in a straight line toward the target, keeping the elbow close to the body (figure 9-18), and strikes the target in a horizontal position (figure 9-19). The front hand positions itself in a protective manner close to the body. The hip is rotated as far as it will go into the punch, and the rear heel comes off the floor. The weight drops slightly, the front knee bends to a 90-degree angle, and the rear knee bends to maintain a straight-backed body position. The shoulder of the punching arm stays low and does not travel further forward than the hip. Upon completion of the technique, the hip and feet return to a normal front stance, and the hands resume a normal fighting position (figure 9-20). (NOTE: Some styles prefer keeping the rear front flat on the floor, sacrificing some hip rotation and punch extension for greater foot contact with the floor. Figure 9-21 shows this "flat-footed" type of reverse punch.)

Hand Strikes 93

Figure 9.17

Figure 9.18

Figure 9.19

Figure 9.20

Figure 9.21

Vertical Punch

The vertical punch utilizes the same principles as the reverse punch and jab (depending upon whether the rear hand or front hand is used for the strike). However, it is considered a *medium-range* technique, and is used when the distance between the fighters is closer than usual. The fist does not turn palm down, but remains vertical allowing for more power transfer and greater wrist stability at medium range. The striking surface remains the large knuckles of the index and middle fingers (except for the "Wing Chun" type first described earlier).

The beginning position (figure 9-22) is a front stance with hands in a basic fighting position. In figure 9-23, the front hand is used for the strike, with the same upper body rotation and weight shifts as for the "jab" in figures 9-14 - 9-16. Note the distancing to the opponent required for maximum effectiveness of the front hand vertical punch. Figure 9-24 shows the rear hand vertical punch and the distancing required. In this case, the body movement for rotational power is the same as for the reverse punch (figure 9-17 through 9-20). Note also that while using either hand for the punch, the other hand is held high, with the elbow protecting the midsection and the first protecting the face. The finishing position for both front hand and rear hand vertical punches is a return to the front stance and basic fighting position of the hands.

Figure 9.22

Figure 9.23

Figure 9.24

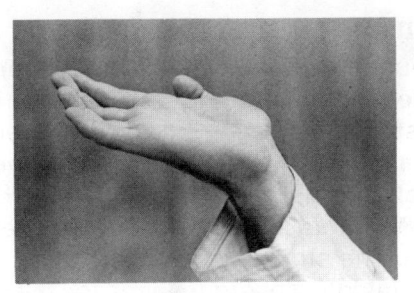

Figure 9.25

KNIFEHAND

Formation of the karate "knifehand" begins with the hand open and flat. The thumb is tucked in against the side of the index finger and bent at the joints as far as possible. The fingers are bent slightly at the middle joint and pulled back towards the back of the hand (figure 9-25). The striking surface of the hand is the outside edge, slightly towards the palm, so that the force of the blow is taken on the padded portion of the hand rather than the bone. The application is generally to an area that requires a thin-edged rather than bulky striking surface.

Several different variations exist for the knifehand strike, all executed from a basic fighting position of the hands:

Inward Strike

The knifehand is held palm up and the wrist is bent at an angle that may vary between 30 and 90 degrees, depending on the distance from the opponent. (Figure 9-25 shows a 45-degree bend for a medium-range strike.) The strike is executed in a "whipping" motion that leads with the elbow and inverts the hand just before striking (similar to throwing a "curve-ball" in baseball). This motion is illustrated in figure 9-26 and 9-27. The usual target area is the side

Figure 9.26

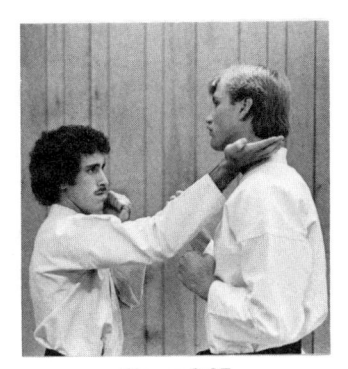

Figure 9.27

Figure 9.28

of the neck or jaw (figure 9-27), or the lower rib area (9-28). This strike is usually executed with the rear hand, and the hip is rotated for power similar to rotation for the reverse-punch motion. The stance used must be the *front* stance.

Outward Strike

The wrist is held straight and the knifehand is palm *down* (figure 9-29), and arm extended (figure 9-31), using primarily the tricep and rear deltoid muscles for power. Target areas include the throat (figure 9-31), ribs, and sides of the neck and jaw. This type of knifehand is executed with the *front* hand.

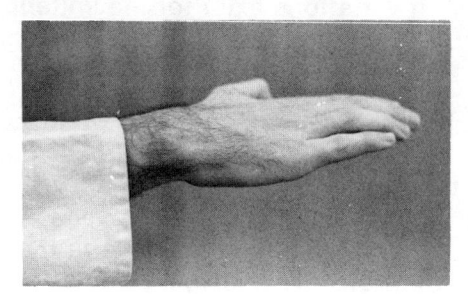

Figure 9.29

Figure 9.30

Figure 9.31

Figure 9.32

Figure 9.33

Figure 9.34

Figure 9.35

Downward Strike

Again the wrist is held straight, but the knifehand is now vertical. The elbow and hand are raised prior to the strike (figure 9-32), and the elbow leads as the strike descends (figure 9-33). Primary targets include the collarbone (figure 9-33) or the back of the neck (on the bent-over opponent, figure 9-34). The weight is dropped on impact, adding considerable force to the strike. The downward strike may be executed with the front (figure 9-33) or rear (figure 9-34) hand, although the rear-hand strike affords more power through hip rotation. If the rear hand is used, a front stance must also be used.

Upward Strike

The upward knifehand strike is generally seen only in self-defense situations against an opponent located to the rear. The target is the groin area (figure 9-35). The upward strike may be from ready, front, or side stances.

98   Hand Strikes

RIDGEHAND

The ridgehand resembles the knifehand, except that the thumb is tucked *under* the hand (figure 9-36), leaving the inner "ridge" of the hand for a striking surface. The wrist is held straight and the target areas include the neck, temple, side of jaw, ribs, or abdomen.

Variations of the ridgehand include the following (all begin from a standard fighting position of the hands):

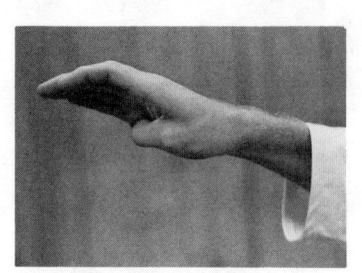

Figure 9.36

Figure 9.37

Figure 9.38

Figure 9.39

Inward

This strike begins from a slightly cocked position (figure 9-37); the arm is held straight and the ridgehand strikes in a palm-down position (figure 9-38). If the rear hand does the striking the stance must be the front stance, and hip rotation provides the power (figure 9-38). If the front hand is used for the strike, either the front stance or the side stance may be used, and upper body rotation is used as the power source (figure 9-39). The inward ridgehand strike is a long-range technique with many of the same applications as the jab or reverse punch, although the target areas are different. The front hand ridgehand from a side stance is a particular favorite among light-contact tournament karate fighters, because it is easily combined with a side-step into a formidable avoidance/counterstrike movement.

Upward

The only real application of the upward ridgehand strike is to the groin. Figure 9-40 shows a possible self-defense from a downed position against a standing attacker. The hand, in this instance, is held vertically.

Figure 9.40

HAMMERFIST

The formation of the hammerfist is identical to the standard karate fist (figures 9-1 through 9-4). The striking surface is the padded part of the hand between the knuckle joint of the little finger and the wrist (figure 9-41). The purpose of this strike is to provide a padded, massive striking area that can provide a concussive effect against a "hard" target, such as the head, side of the jaw, ribs, sternum or face. Begun from a basic fighting position of the hands, variations include:

Figure 9.41

Figure 9.42

Figure 9.43

Inward

In a motion identical to that used to land the inward knifehand strike, the inward hammerfist strike uses hip rotation for power and the wrist is bent according to the distance to the opponent (usually close-to-medium). This inward strike must be executed with the rear hand, and only from a front stance (figures 9-42 and 9-43).

Outward

The motion involved in executing this variation is identical to that for the outward knifehand strike. The wrist is straight, and the fist held palm down. The striking hand is the front hand, and the stance may be either the front (figure 9-44 and 9-45) or the side stance.

Figure 9.44

Figure 9.45

Figure 9.46

Figure 9.47

Figure 9.48

Figure 9.49

Downward

In a motion identical to the downward knifehand strike, the downward hammerfist strike is used against the collarbone (figures 9-46 and 9-47) or back of the neck (against a bent-over opponent, figure 9-48). The front hand hammerfist may be executed from either a front or a side stance (figure 9-47), while the rear hand hammerfist may be executed from a front stance only (figure 9-48). The latter provides more power due to the available hip rotation.

Upward

Used for self-defense situations, the upward hammerfist strike is directed to the groin of an attacker approaching from the rear (figure 9-49). It may be executed from ready front, or side stances.

PALM-HEEL

The palm-heel strike offers the advantage of striking with a larger surface area, thereby reducing the chance of missing the target. The open hand is bent backward at the wrist as far as possible and the fingers are tensed and slightly flexed. The thumb is tucked against the side of the hand (figure 9-50).

Begun from the basic fighting position of the hands, variations include:

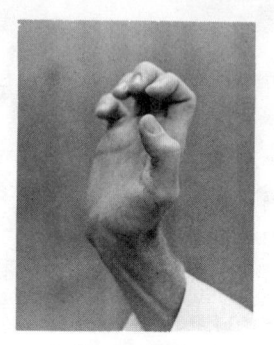

Figure 9.50

Figure 9.51

Figure 9.52

Vertical Palm-Heel

This strike is used for longer-range strikes. If the front hand is used, the motion is identical to that of the jab, and the power comes from upper body rotation and weight shift. Stance may be the front (figure 9-51) or side stance. If the rear hand is used, the motion is identical to that of the reverse punch, with power from hip rotation. In this case the stance must be the front stance (figure 9-52). Targets include the chin (figure 9-51), nose (figure 9-52), or sternum.

Figure 9.53

Figure 9.54

Horizontal Palm-heel

This strike is used for medium-range strikes. The fingers are turned outward 90 degrees, and the striking motion is identical to the vertical punch strike. Targets include the ribs (figure 9-53) and groin (figure 9-54).

The power in all palm-heel strikes is diminished due to the greater surface striking area. Therefore, strikes to the body using the palm-heel should be executed only with the **rear** hand, and from a **front stance** (to allow for hip rotation).

BACKFIST

The backfist strike relies entirely on great speed and body momentum for power, and has a variety of strategic uses. The striking area is the back of the index and middle finger knuckles, which are extended backward due to the bent wrist unique to this type of strike (figure 9-55). The primary use of the backfist is that of a fast, stunning technique executed almost exclusively to the face area.

The speed with which the backfist can be executed has made it a longtime favorite among tournament competitors. It is not uncommon at a modern tournament to see over a quarter of all points scored via backfist strikes.

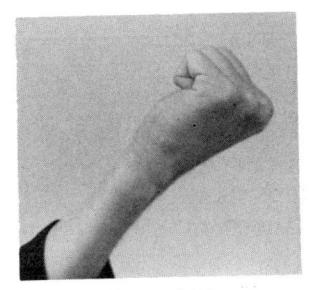

Figure 9.55

Hand Strikes

Variations of the backfist strike include the following:

Outward

Execution of the outward backfist strike is identical to that of the outward knifehand or hammerfist strikes, except for the hand position. From a standard fighting position using the side stance or the front stance, the elbow is raised and pointed at the target (figure 9-56). The arm is straightened, with the back of the index and middle finger knuckles striking the target, which can be the temple (figure 9-57) or the nose.

Figure 9.56

Figure 9.57

Downward

The downward backfist strike is a specialty variation used primarily for one target — the nose. This variation lacks the power of the outward backfist strike due to arm positioning, but can come in handy when the striking arm is already raised, such as following a high block (figures 9-58 and 9-59) or when the target is protected from a horizontal-type strike (figure 9-60). This type of backfist strike may be executed from either a front stance or a side stance. A delivery method should be chosen (see Chapter 14) which will allow maximum power from body momentum, since relatively little power from local muscle or body rotation will be available for either the outward or downward backfist strikes.

Figure 9.58

Figure 9.59

Figure 9.60

FINGER STRIKES

Finger strikes are used strictly as self-defense weapons and are never allowed in any type of competition. The single and two-finger strikes are the finger strikes taught at the beginning level, and are used almost exclusively to the eyes.

Finger strikes are considered to be incapacitating-type strikes that could result in serious injury. For this reason, they are recommended only for self-defense situations in which bodily harm is seriously threatened and possible serious permanent injury to the attacker is warranted.

One-finger strike

This strike is formed by extending the index finger to a nearly straight (but not locked) position. The other fingers are bent at the middle joint and are all pressed together (these serve as "stops" to prevent the striking finger from entering the eye too deeply). The thumb is tucked along the side of the hand to keep it from possible injury. The hand is held vertically with a straight wrist (figure 9-61). The target is a single eye. The front hand is recommended for the strike, since little power is needed and the front hand can reach the target quicker. The motion is similar to the jab (figure 9-62) and can be executed from either a side stance or a front stance.

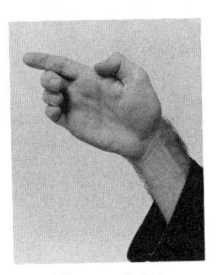

Figure 9.61

Figure 9.62

Two-finger strike

The two finger strike is preferable to the one-finger strike when it is desirable to incapacitate both eyes — generally when there is a need to potentially injure, rather than discourage the attacker.

The hand position (figure 9-63) is similar to the one-finger strike in that the thumb is tucked against the side of the hand, the ring and little fingers are curled at the middle knuckle joint, and the striking fingers are slightly bent (to prevent injury should one miss the eyes). The wrist is again held straight.

The striking motion is identical to that of the one-finger strike, and again the front hand is recommended (figure 9-64). The stance may be either a front or a side stance.

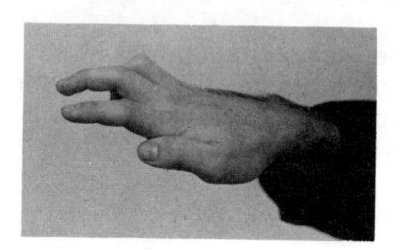

Figure 9.63

Figure 9.64

CHAPTER 9 EVALUATION

Multiple Choice: Circle the letter of the correct answer.
1. The jab is executed with the
   a. front or back hand
   b. back hand only
   c. front hand only
   d. front hand if to the face, back hand if to the body
2. The reverse punch is always executed
   a. with the front hand
   b. with the rear hand
   c. from a side stance, with either hand
   d. to the body, with the rear hand only
3. The vertical punch is designed for use
   a. at close range
   c. at long range
   b. at medium range
   d. at long or medium range
4. Primary target areas for the backfist include
   a. the face and chest areas
   b. the face and groin areas
   c. the face almost exclusively
   d. the chest area almost exclusively
5. Two-finger strikes are used when
   a. a small striking surface is desired
   b. the solar plexus area is being attacked
   c. a board-breaking demonstration is desired
   d. incapacitating both eyes is desirable

Fill in the blanks:
1. The straight punch is also commonly referred to in karate as the _____ punch.

2. Whenever weight shifts or body rotations are incorporated into hand techniques, they must be completed _____ with the hand strike.

3. Some karate styles prefer that the heel of the rear foot be flat on the floor during execution of the reverse punch, sacrificing _____ for greater _____ _____.

Handstrikes

4. The same general body motion used in the jab is also used in the front-hand _____ punch, front-hand _____ strike, and all front hand _____ strikes.

5. Two favorite hand techniques of tournament fighters are the _____ punch and _____ strike.

Questions for Thought and Essay:

Based upon the descriptions of striking surfaces, target areas, and methods of execution described in this chapter, why should the typical karate student develop large protecting calluses on the hands and knuckles?

Chapter 10
Kicks

Front Kick

The front kick is usually the first kick taught since it has fewer body shifts and involves fewer different muscles than most other kicks (therefore being, at least theoretically, *easier* to execute), it clearly illustrates certain principles included in most subsequently-taught kicks, and it blends well with basic hand/foot combinations.

The front kick is used tactically as a fast, linear technique which hits with good power through local muscle use (the primary power muscles, the *quadriceps* group, are quite strong), body momentum, and some hip rotation. Strategically, the front kick can be used *defensively* to stop a charging aggressor and keep them at a distance, *offensively* as a long-range weapon or as part of a linear front kick/hand combination attack.

The front kick is generally used to the solar plexus, abdomen, or groin of an opponent in a front stance. Due to its linear nature, this kick is less effective against an opponent in a side stance. The face is an infrequent target area, although the front kick can be quite effective against an opponent who does a lot of ducking.

The front kick is best executed from a front stance (figure 10-1) and generally utilizes the rear leg for kicking. The knee is raised very high (figure 10-2) in an attempt to create a travel path for the foot that is parallel to the ground. The supporting foot turns outward, and the hands remain in a basic fighting position. The foot is flexed so that the bottom of the foot is parallel to the ground. The

Figure 10.1					Figure 10.2

toes are pulled back toward the knee as far as possible. Upon extension of the leg (figure 10-3 and 10-4) the knee descends downward somewhat, and the ankle straightens, pushing the ball of the foot into the target (figure 10-4). Note that the hip of the kicking leg extends forward adding power and reach through pivotal rotation (figure 10-5), and that this hip extension can only be accomplished if the supporting foot is properly rotated outward. Note also that the hands remain in a basic fighting position, although they have exchanged positions, and the hand that was in back is now in front.

Figure 10.3

Figure 10.4

Figure 10.5

As soon as full extension (but never locking!) of the leg is reached, the process repeats itself backwards, and the knee returns to the "cocked" position (figure 10-6). The leg may now be placed either forward or backward into another front stance (figure 10-7), or followups with the hands may be executed (see Chapter 15).

Figure 10.6

Figure 10.7

ROUNDHOUSE KICK

The roundhouse, or "round" kick, is extremely versatile, with a variety of targets and angles of execution. It can be executed with either the front or rear leg, and practical target areas include the knees, groin, torso, and head. Power in the kick comes from local quadricep muscles and hip rotation (particularly the back-leg roundhouse). The striking surface may be either the ball of the foot (figure 10-8), or the top of the foot (figure 10-9). The ball of the foot is more penetrating due to the smaller striking area, while the top of the foot offers advantages in reach and toe protection.

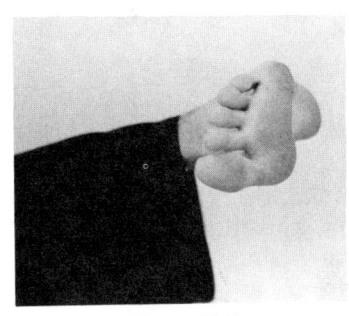

Figure 10.8

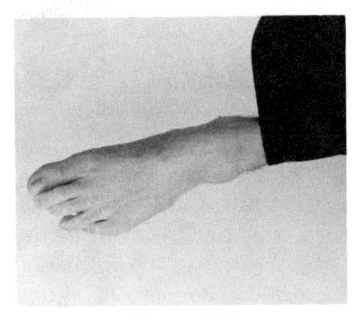

Figure 10.9

112 Kicks

The *back-leg* roundhouse kick is generally executed from a *front* stance (figure 10-10), and is used as a lateral power kick. It is often combined with hand techniques, which are executed *before* the kick, *after* or both. Execution of the kick begins with the raising of the knee simultaneously with the all-important "rolling" of the hip (figure 10-11). When the knee points at the target, the hip has rolled over in line with both legs, and the supporting foot has rotated to point to the rear at least 45 degrees. Notice the hands have switched position, and the body is kept upright with the back slightly arched. The kicking leg extends at the knee, striking with the ball (figure 10-12) or top (figure 10-13) of the foot. (Either striking surface may be used to any of the target areas, although figures 10-12 and 10-13 portray mid-level and high kicks, respectively.)

Figure 10.10

Figure 10.11

Figure 10.12

Figure 10.13

Figure 10.14

Figure 10.15

Figure 10.16

Figure 10.17

Figure 10.18

Figure 10.19

    The leg returns to the loaded position immediately after contact is made (figure 10-14), and usually sets down forward into a front (figure 10-15) or side stance.

    The *front leg* roundhouse kick may begin from either a front or side stance (figure 10-16), or a back stance. The knee rises to point at the target (figure 10-17), and extension of the leg (figure 10-18) completes the motion. Note the body and supporting foot position. Retraction of the leg immediately follows, and the kicking leg is always placed forward into another front or side stance (figure 10-19). The front-leg round kick hits with less power than the back-leg version, but reaches the target *sooner.* In addition, this front-leg kick can, with practice, be executed with great speed, making it a favorite of many tournament and full-contact karate fighters.

The round kick may be executed with different angles of trajectory. The most common are angles of 45 degrees (figures 10-20 and 10-21) or 90 degrees (figures 10-22 and 10-23), although angles of less than 45 degrees are sometimes seen.

Figure 10.20

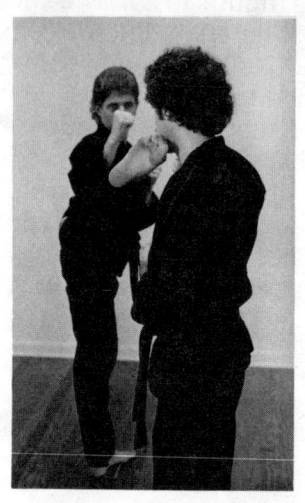

Figure 10.21

Figure 10.22

Figure 10.23

SIDE KICK

The side kick is one of the strongest of all kicks due mainly to the use, at full extension, of the large and powerful *gluteus,* or buttock, muscles. The speed and power that can be generated in the side kick makes it a favorite among martial artists for breaking demonstrations, self-defense movements, and competition (particularly for keeping a larger opponent at a distance).

The side kick is best executed with the *front* leg and from a side stance (figure 10-24). The knee is raised high and to the front (figure 10-25). The ankle is turned to the outside to expose the "blade" of the foot as the striking surface, and the toes are pulled up towards the knee to get them out of the way. The knee should be pulled up toward the chest as much as possible to provide the straightest possible trajectory line into the target. Simultaneously, the supporting foot rotates to a point at least 45 degrees to the rear. In the fully "loaded" position, the striking part of the foot should be in line with both the target and kicker's hip. (Figure 10-26 shows this position from the target's perspective.) The foot travels a straight line

Figure 10.24

Figure 10.25

Figure 10.26

Figure 10.27

Figure 10.28

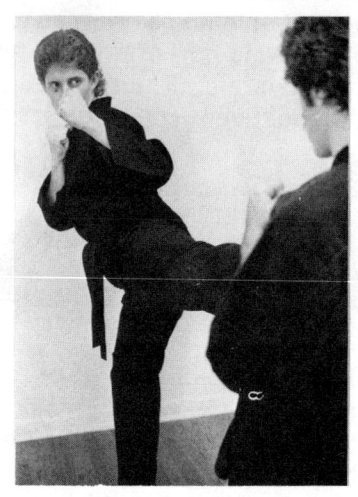

Figure 10.29

towards the target, and care is taken to keep the knee higher than the foot throughout this movement (figures 10-27 and 10-28). At full extension the knee is straightened and the hip of the kicking leg is rotated to the front to incorporate the gluteus muscles to add considerable power to the kick (figure 10-28). (Figure 10-29 shows this last step from the target's perspective. Note the back is arched to allow the kicker to remain as upright as possible, and the hands remain in a fighting position.) The kick is retracted to the loaded position (figure 10-30), and the kicker sets the leg down forward into another front stance (figure 10-31). It is important that the hip not be rotated into the target until the last moment before extension. If rotated sooner, the power generated by this motion will be

Figure 10.30

Figure 10.31

Figure 10.32

dissipated through the extension of the kick. Figure 10-32 illustrates this incorrect method of rolling the hip too soon. Note that the knee dropping below the level of the foot during the extension of the kick is a sure sign of the hip rolling prematurely.

The side kick may also be executed with the *rear* leg from a *front* stance, although this method has fallen into technical disfavor due to the length of time it takes to chamber, or load, the kick. Although not really practical for most fighting uses, the *rear* leg side kick is still seen in some advanced forms.

The primary targets for the side kick are the ribs, solar plexus, or abdomen. Occasionally side kicks may be brought to the head, although power is lost in the upward motion and the kick is easier to block when aimed high.

GROIN KICK

The groin kick is actually a modified version of the front kick. Although it is used mainly to attack the groin, it can also be used to the face or body of an opponent who is bent over. The striking surface is the top of the foot and the toes are bent downward.

The initial motion of the rear-leg groin kick is much like that of the front kick, with the stance being the front stance and the supporting foot turning to the outside. However, the knee is not raised as high and the toes are kept pointing downward. The knee should point at the target to be struck (figures 10-33 and 10-34). The leg simply extends from this point, and the hip flexor and quadriceps muscles combine to produce the power of the kick, along with any forward momentum or rotational power that may be harnessed through the extension of the kicking hip. After striking the target, the kick is retracted (figure 10-35) and set down forward or backward into another front stance.

The front-leg groin kick may be executed from a front, back, or side stance, using the same motions as for the back leg kick. You must remember, however, to shift your weight to the rear supporting leg before raising the front leg to kick.

Figure 10.33

Figure 10.34

Figure 10.35

Figure 10.36

Figure 10.37

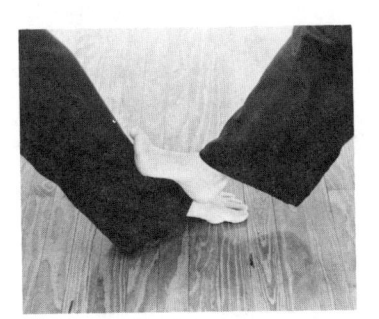

Figure 10.38

Figure 10.39

STOMPING KICK

The stomping kick is easily executed and can land with great power, since nearly all the body weight can be incorporated into the stomp.

This technique has the obvious use of striking a downed opponent. It may also be used against the knee or instep of a standing attacker.

Against the opponent who has been downed from a sweeping technique (see Chapter 13), the knee of the front leg is raised high (figure 10-36) and the heel is brought down on the target area, which should be one of the vital areas (see Chapter 18). The toes are pulled back out of the way and the quadriceps, hamstring, and gluteus muscles contract at extension to lend power to the kick (figure 10-37). An identical kicking motion can be used against the opponent's foot (figure 10-38), shin, or knee (figure 10-39).

CHAPTER 10 EVALUATION

Multiple Choice: Circle the letter of the correct answer.
1. The front kick:
    a. is an offensive weapon
    b. is a defensive weapon
    c. can be used either offensively or defensively
    d. is an offensive short-range weapon
2. The front-leg roundhouse kick is usually executed from:
    a. front, side, or ready stance
    b. side or back stance
    c. front or side stance
    d. front, side, or back stance
3. The side kick is best executed:
    a. with the front leg from a front stance
    b. with the front leg from a side stance
    c. with the back leg from a front stance
    d. with the back leg from a side stance
4. The striking surface of the foot for the side kick is the:
    a. side, or "blade" of the foot
    b. instep
    c. ball
    d. bottom of the heel
5. The knee of the kicking leg should point at the target during the "loaded" position for the:
    a. front and round kicks
    b. round and side kicks
    c. groin and side kicks
    d. round and groin kicks

Fill in the blanks:
1. The front kick is considered _____ to learn than most other kicks.
2. The angles of trajectory most commonly used for the roundhouse kick are the _____ and _____ degree angles, although angles of less than _____ degrees are commonly seen.

122 Kicks

3. The primary targets for the side kick are the _____, _____ and _____, although in some instances the _____ may be attached.

4. The primary target areas for the front kick are the _____, _____, and _____ of the opponent in a front stance. This kick is less effective against an opponent in a _____ stance.

5. The side kick is considered one of the strongest of all kicks, due mainly to the use of the large powerful _____ or _____ muscles.

Chapter 11
Blocks

Forearm Blocks

The forearm blocks are generally the first blocks taught since they require little pre-conditioning or prior karate knowledge. Three major points to remember are:

1. Forearm blocks are redirectional blocks, meaning they do not meet a strike force-on-force, but rather redirect it away from its intended target. They do not stop strikes, but deflect them. Any attempt to stop strikes with forearm blocks may result in the collapse of the blocks.

2. Even redirection of a strike can result in injury to the blocker if performed improperly. To prevent damage to the blocking arm, the part of the forearm that makes contact with the strike must be the *outside* of the forearm on the large muscle mass just below the elbow joint. Making contact with other parts of the arm, particularly the bones on either side of the forearm, can result in serious injury to the blocking arm.

3. Each forearm block is designed to redirect strikes aimed at a particular area. The block must not be shortened or "cropped" in any way which would prevent its covering its assigned area adequately. This is a particular problem with forearm blocks because they pivot from the elbow, and a small deviation in elbow position can result in a major loss of forearm "sweep" area. Forearm blocks may be executed from any stance. The major forearm blocks are as follows:

Low forearm block

This block is designed to cover the lower abdomen and groin area. The block begins with the fist in a palm up position close to

124   Blocks

Figure 11.1

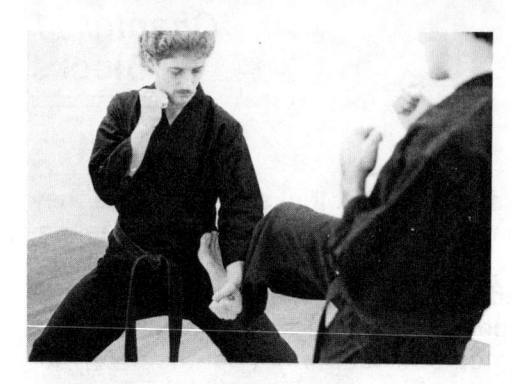

Figure 11.2

Figure 11.3

the body at mid-chest level (figure 11-1). The elbow is also close to the body, and stays that way throughout the block. The arm pivots at the elbow, sweeping the lower body area with the back of the forearm (figure 11-2). As the outside of the forearm reaches the outside of the body, the fist turns palm down (figure 11-3), effectively preventing the strike from slipping down the arm and into the body. Notice the non-blocking hand held high but prepared to counterstrike.

Figure 11.4

Figure 11.5

Figure 11.6

Figure 11.7

High forearm block

This block protects against strikes directed *downward* toward the head region. The blocking hand begins with the fist palm *in* and close to the face. The elbow is also very close to the body (figure 11-4). As the arm begins its upward travel over the head, the fist begins turning palm *out,* and contact with the strike is made with the forearm (figure 11-5). At extension, the fist is palm out, and the arm is positioned as if a *punch* had been executed directly overhead (figure 11-6). Actually, the strike meets the steeply-angled forearm muscle, and slides down and off the body at the shoulder. Finishing position for the block is with the blocking arm dropped back to an angle of approximately 30 degrees (figure 11-7).

Figure 11.8

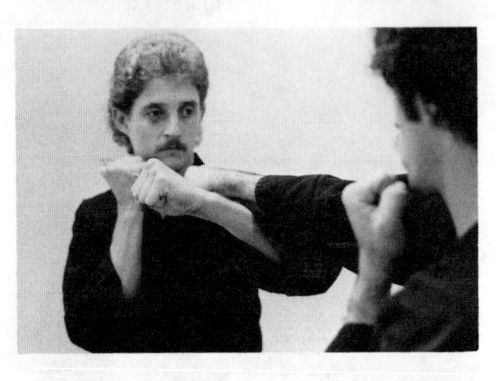

Figure 11.9

Figure 11.10

Outside middle forearm block

The outward middle block protects not only the chest area, but the throat, neck, and face as well. Starting position for the block is similar to the low forearm block except the fist is held palm down (figure 11-8). As the forearm pivots from the elbow, the strike is deflected by the forearm muscle (figure 11-9). Ending position is with the fist turned palm in and a 90-degree bend at the elbow (figure 11-10). (Note that the block can be adjusted to protect either lower or higher simply by changing the height of the elbow before beginning the block.)

Inward middle forearm block

This block protects the same area as the outward middle block, but begins *out*side the body target area and block *inward*. Starting position is with the elbow flared and the fist held palm out (figure 11-11). As the elbow moves inward, a 90-degree elbow bend is maintained and the forearm rotates at the elbow, bringing the forearm muscle in contact with the strike (figure 11-12) and turning the fist palm *inward*. As the elbow moves in front of the body and the forearm continues to rotate, the upper body is also turned in the same direction, so that the deflected strike misses the body entirely (figure 11-13). This block can also be adjusted high or low by changing the elbow height.

Figure 11.11

Figure 11.12

Figure 11.13

OPEN-HAND BLOCKS

Open-hand blocks do not cover as large in area as forearm blocks, nor are they as strong. However, they do offer the advantages of being faster, allowing for grabbing the weapon, and less likelihood of injuring the attacker (applicable in some cases). Again, the open-hand is a *redirectional* block.

Low open-hand block

This motion is similar to that of the low forearm block. The open hand sweeps the strike to the outside of the body, with contact made on the palm of the hand (figures 11-14 and 11-15.) The fingers should be held together rigidly to prevent sprains. Notice that the hip rotates slightly in the direction *away* from the block, making it even easier for the block to sweep the kick past the body. This block is usually executed from the side, front, or back stances.

Figure 11.14

Figure 11.15

Figure 11.16

Figure 11.17

Figure 11.18

Inward open-hand block

In a motion similar to the inward forearm block, the palm of the hand redirects the strike past the face or body, which generally pivots in the opposite direction (figures 11-16 and 11-17). This particular block has a wide range of height adjustments to match areas being attacked (figure 11-18). Side, back or front stances are generally used.

Knife-hand block

Although generally seen done from a back stance, knife-hand blocks are commonly executed from front and side stances as well. The block is usually executed in an *outward* fashion (figure 11-19), or as a *low* block (figure 11-20), although it can also be used as a *high* block (figure 11-21), or an *inward* block (figure 11-22). In all cases, the block is still used to *deflect,* rather than *stop.*

Figure 11.19

Figure 11.20

Figure 11.21

Figure 11.22

CHAPTER 11 EVALUATION

Multiple Choice: Circle the letter of the correct answer.
1. When executing forearm blocks, we must always be careful to make contact with the strike only with the:
   a. inside bone of the forearm
   b. outside bone of the forearm
   c. inside muscle of the forearm
   d. outside muscle of the forearm
2. The inward and outward middle forearm blocks may be adjusted for height by:
   a. beginning the block at a different point
   b. raising or lowering the elbow
   c. raising or lowering the hand
   d. bending the knees and dropping the weight
3. The **high** block protects against:
   a. strikes directed at the face
   b. strikes directed downward at the head
   c. downward strikes or linear kicks to the face
   d. any strike to the upper area
4. The advantages of using open-hand blocks include:
   a. speed
   b. grabbing ability
   c. greater likelihood of injuring attacker
   d. a & b
5. The knife-hand block is commonly executed from the:
   a. front stance   c. side stance
   b. back stance   d. all of the above

Fill in the blank:
1. Most blocks are not really meant to "stop" strikes, but rather to _____ them.

2. The low forearm block is designed to protect the _____ _____ and _____ area.

3. The motion of the low open-block is similar to that of the _____ block.

4. The outward middle block is designed to protect the _____ , _____ , and _____ areas.

Questions for Thought and Essay:
Besides learning how to block strikes, the martial artist develops the ability to *avoid* most strikes. Given the choice between the two, when would it be more advantageous for you as a karate fighter to stand your ground and block rather than move to avoid a strike?

Chapter 12
Use of Elbows and Knees

Elbow and knee strikes are among the most devastating of karate techniques. The bone nature of the joints provides a large, hard, striking surface, and with proper use of muscular and rotational power, tremendous force can be developed in the strikes. The elbow and knee strikes are considered so dangerous that they are not allowed in sport karate and are used strictly for self-defense purposes.

ELBOWS

The two most common elbow strikes include the *upward elbow strike* (figure 12-1) and the *roundhouse elbow strike* (figure 12-2.) These are shown as executed with the rear arm and utilizing hip rotation for power, although the front arm could be used also in

Figure 12.1

Figure 12.2

conjunction with either a *step-through* delivery method (figures 12-3 and 12-4, with upward strike), or a *step-out* delivery method (figures 12-5 and 12-6 with roundhouse strike). The target areas on the opponent include the *chin* for the upward strike, and the *jaw, nose,* or *ribcage* for the roundhouse strike.

Figure 12.3

Figure 12.4

Figure 12.5

Figure 12.6

The *side elbow strike* is also commonly used, and is always executed with the front hand, generally from a side stance (figures 12-7 through 12-9). Care should be taken to *extend* the arm across the front of the body prior to the strike, as shown in figure 12-8, to properly "load" the strike for speed and power. The striking area is the rear of the elbow, and target areas include the *face, side of head or sternum.*

The *rear elbow strike* is usually used against opponents approaching from behind, as in figures 12-10 through 12-12. Note that the arm again extends before striking (figure 12-11), and the body movement for power is a step-back into a front stance (figure 12-12). The striking area is the rear of the elbow and target areas include the *face, sternum* or *ribs.*

Elbows and Knees 135

Figure 12.7

Figure 12.8

Figure 12.9

Figure 12.10

Figure 12.11

Figure 12.12

136 Elbows and Knees

The *downward elbow strike* is used against opponents who have become bent over from a midsection punch or kick (figures 12-13 through 12-15). Great power can be generated in this strike due to the downward motion and body weight that can be brought into the strike. The striking area is again the rear of the elbow, and the target areas include the *back of the head, neck,* or *spine.* These are very vital areas, and *this type of strike should therefore be used only in severe self-defense instances. Severe injury including quadraplegia, or even death, could occur as a result of this strike being executed with full power and deep focus.* The downward elbow strike should therefore never be used casually, irresponsibly, or practiced carelessly. It is strictly banned in all sport competition or classroom freesparring.

Figure 12.13

Figure 12.14

Figure 12.15

Figure 12.16

Figure 12.17

Figure 12.18

KNEES

Like elbow strikes, knee strikes are dangerous, effective, and used strickly for serious self-defense encounters. You should be very careful during practice to avoid making contact with these strikes.

The two basic knee strikes are the *upward strike* (figures 12-16 and 12-17) and roundhouse strike (figure 12-18). Both use the top of kneecap as a striking surface, and the hip flexor muscles as primary accelerators. (The roundhouse knee strike adds the abductor muscles and hip rotation as well). The rear leg is recommended for both strikes, as the knee of the front leg has little distance available between it and the target in which to build velocity. Target areas for the upward strike include the *groin* (figure 12-16) and the face of the bent-over opponent (figure 12-17), while the roundhouse strike generally is used to the midsection (figure 12-18).

One other knee strike bears mentioning. Although known as the *downward knee strike*, it is really just a dropping of the weight, through the knee, on a downed opponent, usually after a sweep. It may be used with devastating results to the *groin, midsection* or *face.*

CHAPTER 12 EVALUATION

Multiple Choice: Circle the letter of the correct answer.
1. The *upward* and *roundhouse* elbow strikes should be executed with:
   a. The rear arm
   b. the front arm
   c. either the front or rear arm
   d. the rear arm from kiba-dachi only
2. The *rear* elbow strike is usually used against opponents:
   a. vulnerable to lower-body strikes
   b. vulnerable to elbow strikes with the *rear* arm
   c. approaching from the rear
   d. after an initial front-hand incapacitating strike
3. The *upward* knee strike is usually executed with the:
   a. front leg
   b. rear leg
   c. either leg
   d. front leg against kicking attack, rear leg against hand attack

Fill in the blanks:
1. The two most common elbow strikes are the _____ and the _____.

2. The two basic knee strikes are the _____ and the _____.

3. When executed with the rear arm, elbow strikes use _____ _____ for a power source.

Questions for Thought and Essay:
Elbow and knee strikes are said to be too dangerous for use in other than a "serious" self-defense encounter. How would you know if you were in an encounter "serious enough" to use these strikes?

Chapter 13
Breakfalls and Sweeps

BREAKFALLS

Breakfalling techniques are necessary to prevent injuries from inadvertent falls or being swept. The basic concept behind breakfalling skills is to take the impact of the fall on an area of the body that is the least likely to be injured, such as the outer thigh, and to dissipate as much of the shock as possible through rolling and slapping techniques.

Rear

Although used less in actual practice than the side breakfall, the rear breakfall is the first taught and best illustrates the principles used in all breakfalling techniques.

From a squatting position, with the arms crossed in front of the body and the palms facing outward (figure 13-1), allow yourself to fall backward, contacting the ground first with your buttocks (figure 13-2). Tuck your chin in toward your chest, pull your knees up, and bend your upper body forward, creating a rounded back surface on which to roll. Keep in mind that the areas you wish to protect from hard shock are the spine and back of the head. At the moment you contact the ground with your buttocks, uncross your arms and slap the floor with your palms and forearms on each side of your body. You should have about a 45-degree angle between your arms and your body (figure 13-2). Continue rolling back, allowing the roll to

Figure 13.1

Figure 13.2

Figure 13.3

take up much of the shock of the fall (figure 13-3). Do not allow your arms to remain on the floor; instead rebound them off after they have completed their slap.

Side

The side breakfall is the most commonly used, since most takedowns leave you falling somewhat on the side of your body. The areas to protect include the side of the knee, the hip bones, the ribs and shoulder, and the side of the head.

From a standing position, begin the fall on your right side by collapsing your left leg and bringing your straightened right leg up off the floor. The right arm should be in front of the body for protection (figure 13-4). Make contact with the floor with the outside of your right thigh above the knee, and slap the floor with your right palm at the same time (figure 13-5). Continue to roll on your side up your shoulder (figure 13-6). Keep the chin tucked to the chest to protect your head.

Figure 13.5

Figure 13.4

Figure 13.6

Figure 13.7

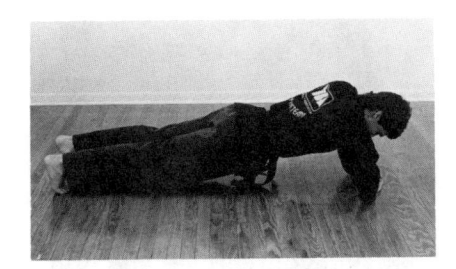

Figure 13.8

Front

Front falls usually happen because of slips or inadvertent trips. Few sweeping techniques are designed to drop the opponent on his or her face, but slips and loss of balance can occur during freefighting practice.

The areas to protect most are the face, chest, and abdomen. As you fall forward, shift your weight to the balls of your feet and extend both arms to the front until the elbows are bent at about a 30-degree angle (figure 13-7). The hands should be palm out, and the fingertips turned inward slightly. Contact with the floor should be made with the palms of the hands only, and the elbows should bend to take up the shock. This bending should stop, obviously, at a point before the face or body would make contact with the floor (figure 13-8).

SWEEPING

Sweeping techniques are designed to compromise an opponent's fighting abilities by removing his or her base of support. Sometimes sweeps are used merely to unbalance an opponent, rendering the opponent more susceptible to attacks or counterattacks. At other times, the object is to take the opponent to the floor, where he or she should be an easy target for an incapacitating strike.

Front Leg

The offensive front leg sweep begins from a standard fighting position (figure 13-9). The sweep is set up by directing the opponent's attention with a hand strike, usually to the face (figure 13-10). The rear leg executes the sweep, making contact with the opponent's ankle with the bottom part of the instep (figures 13-11 and 13-12). The sweeping leg is bent slightly at the knee, but the motion of the technique is an inward sweep of the leg using the *adductor* (inner thigh) muscles. Notice the hands remain high during the sweep to protect against counterattacks. While the opponent is unbalanced, the follow-up, usually a rear hand punch to the body (figure 13-13), is executed.

Figure 13.9

Figure 13.10

Figure 13.11

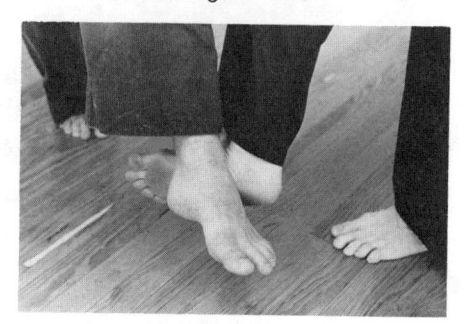

Figure 13.12

Figure 13.13

Breakfalls and Sweeps 145

The front leg-foot sweep may also be executed in a *defensive* manner. From a basic fighting position, the opponent attacks with a jab (figure 13-14). As the opponent's weight is shifted to the front foot, the defender sweeps that foot with his or her rear leg (figure 13-15). As the opponent goes down, the follow-up is executed with either a hand technique (figure 13-16) or a stomping kick (figure 13-17).

Figure 13.14

Figure 13.15

Figure 13.16

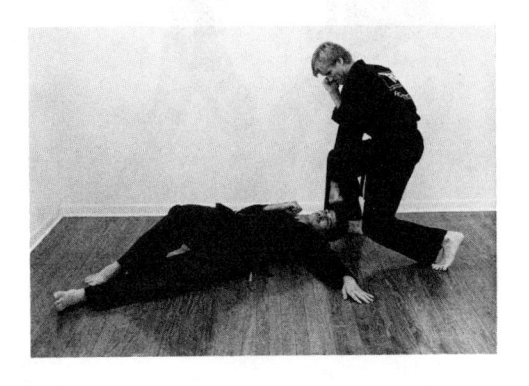

Figure 13.17

146 Breakfalls and Sweeps

Rear Leg

Sweeping of the rear leg produces a result greatly different from that of a front leg sweep. The opponent *always* goes down, and usually very hard. Keep in mind that you are taking out your opponent's only means of weight support, and the opponent therefore assumes a near horizontal position several feet off the ground. When practicing this technique, be certain your partner has received proper training in breakfalls and that you are working on a padded surface.

The idea behind the setup for *offensive use* of this sweep is to get the opponent moving to the rear, usually with an attack involving hand techniques (figure 13-18). As the opponent shifts his weight onto his rear leg, the attacker's rear leg is used to execute the sweep (figure 13-19). The follow-up may be either a hand technique (figure 13-20) or a stomping kick.

Figure 13.18

Figure 13.19

Figure 13.20

Breakfalls and Sweeps 147

The rear leg sweep is used *defensively* as a counter to an opponent's kicking attack. In the example, the opponent's front kick is blocked with a low open hand block, which redirects the kick to the outside of the body (figure 13-21). The opponent's supporting leg is then swept out by the defender's rear leg (figure 13-22), and an appropriate follow-up is effected (figure 13-23).

Figure 13.21

Figure 13.22

Figure 13.23

CHAPTER 13 EVALUATION

Multiple Choice: Circle the letter of the correct answer.
1. The reason for slapping the floor with the palms and forearms during breakfalls is to:
   a. help stabilize body movement
   b. help absorb the shock of the fall
   c. prepare for regaining one's footing
   d. scare the opponent
2. The most commonly used breakfall is the:
   a. standing   c. rolling
   b. rear   d. side
3. The *front leg sweep* may be executed:
   a. in a defensive manner only
   b. offensively or defensively
   c. in an offensive manner only
   d. neither offensively nor defensively
4. The follow-up to the rear leg sweep may be a:
   a. hand technique only
   b. foot technique only
   c. hand or foot technique (usually a stomping kick)
   d. roundhouse kick or hand technique
5. The rear leg sweep is used defensively as:
   a. a counter to the opponent's sweeping attack
   b. a counter to the opponent's punching attack
   c. the initial move of a 3-sweep combination
   d. a counter to the opponent's kicking attack

Fill in the blanks:
1. Breakfalls are needed to prevent injuries that could occur from either _____ techniques or _____ _____.

2. The areas to protect from hard shock when executing a rear breakfall include the _____ and the _____.

3. The areas to protect when executing a side breakfall include the _____, the _____ and _____, and the _____.

4. During execution of a sweep the hands remain _____ to protect against counterattacks.

5. To properly execute a rear leg sweep *offensively*, the opponent's weight must be shifted to his _____ leg.

Questions for Thought and Essay:
What defensive movements can you think of that would be most effective at foiling front leg sweeping attempts?

Chapter 14
Body Movement

DELIVERING ATTACKS

In karate, the idea of "delivering an attack" is synonymous with "closing the distance" — meaning, of course, the distance between you and your opponent. This distance is referred to as the "critical distance," because it is extremely important that a *particular distance be maintained,* both to facilitate your own attack and to prevent you from being easily caught by a surprise attack from your opponent.

The critical distance to maintain is the distance at which you and your opponent are just outside each other's reach using your longest range front-leg technique. (The rear leg could still reach the target, but would be slower and easier to see coming, giving more reaction time. A rear-leg kick is considered a *distance-closing* tactic.) Figure 14-1 shows the proper critical distance to maintain.

It is necessary to close this critical distance to score on the opponent. This can be done for hand techniques by "stepping through" or "stepping out." For kicks, the distance can be closed by kicking with the rear leg, "jumping in" with a front leg kick, or sliding with a front or rear leg kick.

Figure 14.1

Hand Techniques

Step-through. This technique is achieved by stepping forward with the rear foot and delivering a hand technique as soon as the distance is closed. The landing of the hand technique should coincide with the end of the step, to maximize power through utilization of body mass (see Chapter 8).

As you step-through, take care to stay at the same height (rather than rising up in mid-step and then dropping your weight back down), and step with a feel of "moving from the hips", almost as if you were being pulled along by the belt. Let your legs move forward because they are attached to your hips, rather than stepping with your feet and having your body follow along. While this is an abstract idea, it is very important to maintain proper form and positioning of your body's weight and center of gravity. Figures 14-2 through 14-4 illustrate this step-through in conjunction with a jab. The step-through works best with a *front* stance.

Figure 14.2

Figure 14.3

Figure 14.4

Step-out. This is an advanced and very fast way of closing the gap. This method has found great favor among tournament competitors, who use it almost exclusively to deliver front hand jabs, backfists, and reverse punches. Although not as much body momentum is built up as with a step-through, the step-out delivery method is much faster and, with proper timing and speed, a front-hand strike executed with a step-out is nearly impossible to block.

Figure 14-5 shows the beginning position as a front stance with the hands in a standard fighting position. The weight is shifted forward and the front foot is raised slightly from the floor to allow a step-out (figure 14-6). The rear foot is dragged along as the body moves forward. Again, the feeling is that of moving from the hips. The strike should land simultaneously with the planting of the front foot. Figure 14-7 shows this technique as a jab, while figure 14-8

Figure 14.5

Figure 14.6

Figure 14.7

Figure 14.8

shows a reverse punch as the strike. Figures 14-9 and 14-10 illustrate the same step-out delivery method as applied to a side stance and backfist strike.

Notice in each example that the hand not striking is kept high to guard against counterattacks, and the head is moved slightly to one side to take it out of the path any such counterattack would be expected to follow.

Figure 14.9

Figure 14.10

Kicks

Rear-leg. This obviously closes the distance in the same way as stepping toward would. However, *at the moment the distance is closed,* the technique, usually a front or roundhouse kick, lands on *the target.* The kick should score to any good target area if the kick is fast enough to catch the opponent before he or she moves back or blocks. Care should be taken to keep your hands up to prevent counter-strikes in mid-kick. Use front, side, or back stances. This kick is a favorite delivery method of full-contact karate fighters because of the power that can be generated in the kick.

Jump-in. This tactic is usually used to deliver front-leg kicks. Often, a front hand feint precedes the kick.

Figure 14-11 shows the beginning position as a front stance with the hands in a basic fighting position. The rear foot hops forward to replace the front foot as the front leg raises to kick (in this case, a front kick, although other kicks could also be used), and thus the distance is closed. (Although the technical term is a "jump-in", the rear foot does not leave the ground but actually slides up instead.) Figure 14-12 shows the rear foot and front leg in position after the jump-in is completed, and figure 14-13 shows the completed front kick strike. Figures 14-14 through 14-15 illustrate this method used from a side stance to deliver a side kick.

Figure 14.11

Figure 14.12

Figure 14.13

Figure 14.14

Figure 14.15

Figure 14.16

Figure 14.17

Figure 14.18

Slide. This is the fastest of the kick delivery methods. Although not as much power can be generated as in the other two methods, the slide is a particular favorite of tournament fighters, who score often with roundhouse and side kicks delivered by this method.

Figure 14-16 shows the fighters squared off at each other with a proper critical distance between them. The stances are side stances, although a front or back stance would be a better choice if a front kick were the kick to be delivered. The weight is shifted forward for the kick, which is a front-leg kick (although the slide method can also be combined with a rear leg kicking attack.) As the round kick speeds toward its target, the fighter allows momentum to pull him forward, while at the same time he "pushes off" with the toes of his supporting (rear) foot (figure 14-17). When the slide is completed, the kick should be at the target (figure 14-18).

DEFENSIVE BODY MOVEMENT

Body movement as a defense against attack really means one of two things: *widening the distance* between yourself and the opponent, or *moving out of the path* of the attack. The former is accomplished by a "rear step-through," "jump-back," or "step-back" and the latter by what is known as "side-stepping."

Figure 14.19

Figure 14.20

Figure 14.21

Rear step-though. As the name suggests, this method is simply the reverse of the "step-through" attack method. As the opponent advances (it could be any type of attack), the defender simply steps back with the front foot, effectively reestablishing the critical distance (figures 14-19 and 14-20). This method works, but has the disadvantage of being too slow for very fast step-out hand strikes or slide kicks. It does, however, leave you in a good position for counter-attacking once the step-back is completed (figure 14-21).

158   **Body Movement**

Figure 14.22

Figure 14.23

Figure 14.24

Jump-back. The opposite of the "jump-in," this gap-widening method involves stepping back with the front foot followed quickly by a step-back with the rear foot (figures 14-22 through 14-24). It is a quicker method than the rear step-through, although a counter strike cannot be effected until the rear foot reestablishes contact with the floor. This is the best defensive movement using the front or side stances.

Step-back. This is the opposite of the "step-out" and best method to use from the back stance. (To use this method from a front or side stance, the stance must be altered so that the center of gravity and weight are nearly over the rear leg, and the stance is *shorter* than normal. The rear foot simply steps *back*, and the body drags the front foot with it (figures 14-25 through 14-27). Counter strikes must wait until the back foot is planted.

Figure 14.25

Figure 14.26

Figure 14.27

160   Body Movement

Side-Stepping. This is an advanced and desirable defensive movement, since the opponent is automatically set up for a counterattack, with no critical distance for the defender to have to re-close.

Figures 14-28 and 14-29 show a front-leg sidestep in which the defender steps just far enough to the side to avoid the attack (in this case a jab). The attacker is well set up for a counter (figure 14-30). Figures 14-31 and 14-32 show a *rear-leg* sidestep, in this instance against a front kick. The rear leg moves the defender counterclockwise out of the path of the strike (figure 14-31) and into a new stance from which to counter, which in this case happens to be a side stance with a side-kick counterstrike (figure 14-32).

Figure 14.28

Figure 14.29

Figure 14.30

Figure 14.31

Figure 14.32

CHAPTER 14 EVALUATION

Multiple Choice: Circle the letter of the correct answer.
1. "Critical distance" refers to the distance:
   a. needed to effect most counterstrikes.
   b. your feet must travel from the center line for effective side-steps
   c. you do *not* want to maintain between you and the opponent
   d. between you and the opponent
2. When using the "step-out" delivery method, the rear foot:
   a. moves forward past the front foot into a new stance
   b. moves first, *then* the front foot moves
   c. is dragged by the body as it moves forward
   d. does not move until the attack is completed
3. The "jump-in" delivery method is usually used to deliver:
   a. rear-leg kicks   c. rear-hand techniques
   b. front-leg kicks   d. front-hand techniques
4. The fastest of the kick-delivery methods is the:
   a. jump-in   c. rear-leg
   b. slide   d. kick-through
5. The rear foot moves first on which defensive movement:
   a. step-through   c. jump-back
   b. step-out   d. step-back

Fill in the blanks:
1. The idea of "delivering an attack" is really synonymous with "_____ the _____."

2. Delivery methods for hand techniques include the _____ and the _____.

3. Delivery methods for kicks include the _____, _____, and _____.

4. All techniques should land _____ with the conclusion of the delivery method.

5. The best gap-widening defense to use from the cat stance would be the _____.

Questions for Thought and Essay:

Why do we execute sliding front-leg front kicks preferentially from a front or back stance rather than a side stance? Why are the side and roundhouse slide kicks best done from the side stance?

Chapter 15
Combinations (Putting Your Attack Together)

The idea of grouping several techniques into *combinations* was developed with several goals in mind. First, it enables a fighter to land several strikes in quick succession, effecting proportionately greater damage on the opponent. Second, combinations provide a way to open up an opponent's defense with a lead technique and to follow with a power strike in the open area. (Sometimes the lead technique is not really meant to land, but simply is a fake intended to *look* like a real strike and draw the opponent's attention away from the real target area.) Third, combinations enable the fighter to *keep* an opponent on the defensive. The opponent cannot very well counterattack if he or she is frantically trying to block rapid-fire techniques, and if the combination attack is continued, you are sure to land telling strikes sooner or later.

HAND COMBINATIONS

Combination attacks using the hands involve precise applications of speed, timing, and power. The following common hand combination attacks illustrate those points:

Front hand/back hand. A very basic combination, the front hand/back hand is nonetheless extremely effective, and is the classic example of the "one-two" type of attack seen often in box-

164 Combinations

ing as well as karate. The techniques used most often are the *jab* and the *reverse punch*. In figure 15-1, both fighters are in a basic fighting position. The initial move is a *step-out* delivery method with the jab (figure 15-2). The gap must be closed quickly with the step-out and the jab must land simultaneously with the stopping of the forward momentum to provide maximum power to the strike. As soon as the jab is extended, the reverse punch begins speeding toward a facial target (figure 15-3) or to the midsection (figure 15-4). A variation of this attack is to use the front hand strike as a *fake* rather than an actual strike. In this case, the jab is made in a slightly slower and highly animated fashion to draw maximum *reaction* from the opponent. When the opponent does react and raises the arms to block (figure 15-5), the reverse punch is used to strike the exposed midsection area (figure 15-6).

Figure 15.1

Figure 15.2

Figure 15.3

Figure 15.4

Figure 15.5

Figure 15.6

Of course, other appropriate techniques could be used in place of the jab and reverse punch when executing the front hand/back hand type of combination. A jab/ridgehand (figures 15-7 and 15-8) combination works well against the opponent who leaves the side of the head or jaw open when blocking the jab. A palm-heel strike to the chin could open the throat area for a four-finger strike (figures 15-9 and 15-10), and the two-finger strike to the eyes could prelude a knifehand strike to the neck (figures 15-11 and 15-12).

Figure 15.7

Figure 15.8

Figure 15.9

Figure 15.10

166 Combinations

Figure 15.11

Figure 15.12

The front hand/back hand combination can also be directed strictly to the body. Figures 15-13 and 15-14 illustrate two vertical punches directed to the solar plexus.

This combination may also be done with *elbow strikes* rather than hand techniques. A lead-arm side elbow strike (figure 15-15) is an excellent lead-in to a follow-up roundhouse elbow strike to the jaw (figure 15-16).

Figure 15.13

Figure 15.14

Figure 15.15

Figure 15.16

Back hand/front hand. Although much less commonly seen than the front hand/back hand combination, back hand/front hand combination strikes are used when a back-hand power lead is desired, and are particularly effective against opponents conditioned to seeing the front hand/back hand combination. Again, the initial move is a step-out with back-hand hip rotation, followed by upper body rotation into a front-hand strike. Figures 15-17 and 15-18 use a reverse punch and face jab as example techniques.

The back-hand/front-hand combination with the back hand executed as a fake works particularly well, since most opponents expect either a front hand/back hand attack or a one-shot attack. Figure 15-19 shows the reverse punch executed as a fake. Notice the hip is not committed (rotated) into the technique all the way; rather, it is turned only enough to make it "look good." "Saving" the hip this way enables a faster, easier subsequent move into the follow-up jab to the face (figure 15-20).

Figure 15.17

Figure 15.18

Figure 15.19

Figure 15.20

Figure 15.21

Figure 15.22

Figure 15.23

Double front-hand. Executing two or more strikes with the same hand (usually the front hand) is a tactic that uses both speed and deception as primary ingredients. The initial move, in this case, is a jab combined with a step-out delivery method (figure 15-21). As the first jab is withdrawn, the back foot slides up (figure 15-22) in preparation for another step-out jab (figure 15-23).

The key to making this work is the speed at which the second jab is initiated. If there is too much delay, the opponent will have time to react to the second jab. The idea is to have the opponent react to the *first* one, and then relax his guard in time to get hit with the second strike.

This double front-hand combination works not only with the jab, although that strike is commonly seen, but also with any other hand technique you may desire to use.

Multiple hand techniques. Combination strikes involving three or more consecutive hand techniques are advisable under certain circumstances. Although a major aim of karate training is to be able to end a conflict with one strike, this may not always be practical. An opponent able to withstand a strong power strike, or one whose defense does not lend itself to landing a lone technique or one-two combination, is a prime target for a multi-technique combination.

Each individual hand strike may not be as powerful as a single, go-for-broke haymaker, but the result may be a greater chance of landing the technique and achieving the desired result.

The techniques chosen for multi-strike combinations should be those which complement one another; i.e., each strike sets the opponent up for the next one. Figures 15-24 through 15-27 show a series of hand techniques designed to run down a fleeing opponent. The initial move is a step-out jab/reverse punch (figures 15-24 and 15-25). During the reverse punch the back foot begins to slide forward in preparation for another step-out jab (figure 15-26) followed by a ridgehand strike (figure 15-27).

Figure 15.24

Figure 15.25

Figure 15.26

Figure 15.27

Figure 15.28

Figure 15.29

Figure 15.30

HAND/FOOT COMBINATIONS

Combinations involving both hands and feet serve either to take into account changes in critical distance (as in the first example), or to deceive the opponent (as in the second example).

Figures 15-28 through 15-30 show a simple combination involving a back leg front kick (figure 15-28 designed to close the distance and bring the opponent's hands down) followed by a jab/reverse punch hand combination (figures 15-29 and 15-30). The effect of going low-high-low with techniques is the creation of obvious defensive problems for the opponent.

A different approach is illustrated in figures 15-31 through 15-33. Begin by closing the distance with a **jump-in** delivery method designed to close the gap while preparing for a front-leg kick. Along with this jump-in, execute a jab (figure 15-31) bringing the opponent's hands up and leaving the midsection unprotected. The front kick strikes to this area (figure 15-32) followed by a reverse punch (figure 15-33). A similar sequence is seen in figures 15-34 through 15-36, but from a side stance, and using a backfist, side kick, and ridgehand.

Combinations 171

Figure 15.31

Figure 15.32

Figure 15.33

Figure 15.34

Figure 15.35

Figure 15.36

172   Combinations

Figure 15.37

Figure 15.38

Another common distance-closing combination is the step-out hand lead (figure 15-37) followed by a back leg kick, particularly a roundhouse combined with a slide (figure 15-38).

An almost limitless number of hand/foot combinations can be put together using the various stances, techniques, and delivery methods known at this point. Take time to experiment with different combinations and practice them until you can execute them regularly with effectiveness.

COMBINATION KICKS

Kicks executed as a *combination* are usually thought of as kicks *executed with the same leg.* Although these are usually considered as intermediate level techniques, certain simple combination kicks using the kicking techniques already described are included below.

Double-kicks.   The front, round, and side kicks are all suitable for use when "double kicking." In figure 15-39 the front kick is blocked by the opponent. As the opponent begins to counterattack, the front kick is retracted (figure 15-40) and repeated without setting the foot

Figure 15.39

Figure 15.40

Combinations   173

Figure 15.41

down (figure 15-41). Figures 15-42 through 15-44 show the roundhouse kick being directed to different body levels (low and high) as a deception move. The two kicks could also be directed to the same level, or in a high-low fashion. Figures 15-45 through 15-47 show a low-high double-up using a side kick and a roundhouse kick.

At the advanced levels, this same motion and theory is often used to execute three, or even four kicks without setting the foot down.

Figure 15.42

Figure 15.43

Figure 15.44

174   Combinations

Figure 15.45

Figure 15.46

Figure 15.47

CHAPTER 15 EVALUATION

Multiple Choice: Circle the letter of the correct answer.
1. Which of these is *not* a goal of executing a *combination*?
    a. to land several strikes in quick succession for greater damage to the opponent
    b. to keep the opponent on the defensive
    c. to effect a counter strike always after an opponent's attack
    d. to open up an opponent's defense for a power strike by leading with a fake or initial strike
2. The front hand/back hand combination is used:
    a. only with punches
    b. very seldom as a combination
    c. only as a facial attack
    d. with many different hand techniques as options
3. A back hand/front hand combination could be the:
    a. jab/reverse punch
    b. reverse punch/jab
    c. backfist/reverse punch
    d. jab/backfist
4. Multi-technique combinations are particularly advisable against opponents who:
    a. are able to withstand strong power strikes
    b. are able to counterattack very well after an initial strike
    c. are able to defend well against a lone technique or one-two combinations
    d. a & c
5. In a combination using a jump-in roundhouse kick to the body followed by reverse punch to the head, we should:
    a. close the gap with the jump-in, and score with one or both of the techniques we are executing
    b. close the gap with the jump-in, and score only with the roundhouse kick (the reverse punch would be a fake)
    c. break up a kicking attack initiated by the opponent
    d. none of the above

Fill in the blanks:
1. Combination attacks with the hands involve precise applications of _____, _____, and _____ in order to be effective.

2. In order to change a jab (or other technique) into a *fake,* the technique should be done in a slightly _____ and highly _____ fashion.

3. The double front-hand combination uses _____ and _____ as primary ingredients.

4. Techniques chosen for multi-strike combinations should be chosen with the idea in mind that each strike should set the opponent up for _____ _____.

5. Hand/foot combinations serve either to _____ the opponent, or to take into account changes in _____.

Questions for Thought and Essay:
We have examined techniques that work all together in combination. Which techniques do you think would *not* work well together, and why?

Chapter 16
Getting Your Defense Together

Defense, in karate, implies two things: avoiding being hit and preventing the opponent from continuing the attack. The first is accomplished by either *blocking, avoiding,* or *jamming* the opponent's attack. The second is accomplished by always *counterattacking.* Counter-attacking places the opponent on the defensive and prevents a second attack. We will examine counterattacks as inseparable companions to all defensive movements.

BLOCKING

Blocking is the best defense to use against strikes that arrive very quickly and preclude evasive movement. Blocking is also preferred when attempting to open the opponent up for a counter or maintaining your own body position. Figure 16-1 shows an open-hand block being used to deflect a jab that has arrived with such speed as to prevent an avoidance tactic. Figures 16-2 and 16-3 demonstrate how a knife-hand block can "open up" a line of counterattack to an opponent.

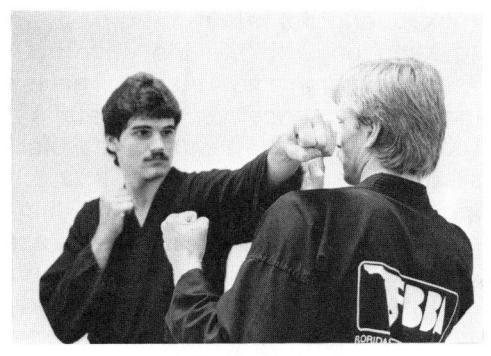

Figure 16.1

178   Defense

Figure 16.2

Figure 16.3

Occasionally a linear movement, usually to the rear, accompanies the block. It may be in the form of a *rear step through, jump-back* or *step-back* (Chapter 14). The block must be executed as the gap-widening movement occurs, rather than after. In other words, the block should begin immediately, since there is a strike coming that must be blocked, and the feet moving back into a new stance should strive to keep up with the block, rather than the block waiting for the feet to assume a new stance. This is a common problem with beginners overly concerned with details of executing the stepping and blocking motions. Holding the block until the rear step-through is completed only results in a *late* block and being struck by the opponent (figure 16-4 and 16-5). Figures 16-6 and 16-7 show a rear step-through/outside forearm block executed with proper timing. Figures 16-8 through 16-10 show a similar tactic using a step back/inside forearm block/reverse punch counter sequence. The gap-widening rear movement gains distance that may be helpful in executing the counterattack.

Defense 179

Figure 16.4

Figure 16.5

Figure 16.6

Figure 16.7

Figure 16.8

Figure 16.9

Figure 16.10

AVOIDING THE ATTACK

Avoidance techniques actually fall into one of two categories — *sidestepping,* and *slipping.* **Sidesteps,** as examined in Chapter 14, are very useful for combining an avoidance movement with the assumption of a new stance suitable for a strong counterattack. As seen in figures 14-28 through 14-32, both front and back-leg sidesteps may be combined with a variety of blocks and counter techniques designed to retake the offensive and break up the opponent's attack.

Slipping techniques look similar but are actually very different from side-steps. When executing a *slip, only the body part being attacked moves;* therefore, the slip is *faster* than a sidestep and does not take the defender out of position nearly as much. This may be very important, depending upon the type of counterattack planned. Figure 16-11 shows a head slip response to a step-out jab. Notice that the feet remain stationary, while only the target (in this case, the head) moves. Figure 16-12 shows how this slip could be combined with a front-hand jab counter, while figure 16-13 shows a slip to the other direction with a body-punch counter. Figure 16-14 illustrates how a slip technique could be applied to an attack to the body, with an outside knifehand strike as a counterattack.

Figure 16.11

Figure 16.12

Figure 16.13

Figure 16.14

JAMMING

This is a very different type of defensive movement from a block, sidestep, or slip. The jamming technique attempts to defuse an opponent's attack before it really reaches the dangerous stage. It meets an attack with what is really another attack. Figure 16-15 shows a jamming side-kick executed against a step-out reverse punch attack. The kick stops the opponent before he really gets close enough to land the punch. In figure 16-16 the attack is a side-kick, but is "jammed" by the defender's own step-out backfist attack.

The decision of whether to block, avoid, or jam an attack really depends on strategic factors that can only be answered through experience. How fast is the opponent? Does the opponent use mainly linear attacks, such as jabs and front or side kicks, lending well to side-steps or slips? Or does the opponent favor lateral attacks, such as ridgehands and round kicks that must be dealt with by widening the gap or blocking? And how fast are you as a blocker or counterattacker? Can you stick that side kick in there as a jam technique before the opponent can step-out reverse punch you? These questions can only be answered by developing your technique to basic proficiency and by experimenting. This experimentation generally involves examination of self-defense applications and free-sparring, which are covered in Chapters 18 and 19 respectively.

Figure 16.15

Figure 16.16

CHAPTER 16 EVALUATION

Fill in the blanks:

1. When talking about *defense* in karate, we are really talking about keeping from _____ _____, and executing an effective _____ technique.

2. The three ways to avoid getting hit are to _____, use an _____ technique, or use a _____ technique.

3. Blocks are often accompanied by a linear defensive movement to the rear, executed as a _____-_____ technique designed to provide some room for counter-attacking.

Questions for Thought and Essay:
Why would it be unwise to attempt to specialize in one type of defensive movement, say blocking or sidestepping, to the exclusion of the others, even if near-perfection could be attained with that specialty movement?

Chapter 17
Forms-Practicing for Perfection

A martial arts *form* is a prearranged, choreographed, imaginary fight against either single or multiple opponents. Some forms include only elementary techniques and are designed for beginners, while others contain more difficult techniques and are practiced by the intermediate and advanced students.

HISTORY AND BENEFITS

Many forms practiced today were developed centuries ago in the Orient. These forms typically included the favorite techniques of the authoring instructor and sometimes even described an actual confrontation the instructor had experienced. Many forms are known by the name of the developer, such as the popular Okinawan forms *Kushanku* and *Wanchu.* (These men were Chinese military representatives assigned to Okinawa in the 1700s). Others are named for the location at which they were developed, such as the *Nahanchi* form (for the old Okinawan port city of *Naha*) or *Koryo* from (the ancient name for present-day Korea). Still others of the traditional forms have oriental names that relate specific meanings. *Bassai,* a form very popular among most Japanese, Korean, and Okinawan styles means literally "to penetrate a fortress," implying that the form contains movements that are difficult to defend against. The intermediate forms of most Japanese styles belong to the *Pinan* or *Heian* series, which both mean "peaceful mind," a condition of confidence which it is hoped the students who master these forms will achieve.

Some forms are not ancient in origin at all, but were developed in recent years to keep pace with developing needs. The American karate styles generally practice recently-developed forms, and top national forms competitors are constantly reworking old forms or putting together new ones in an attempt to "show their best" to the judges.

Despite these diversities, the basic idea behind all training forms remains the same: the form offers the student a chance to practice stances, blocks, hand strikes, kicks, and body movement in a manner that is more realistic and interesting than simple over-and-over repetitions. Forms were particularly important in ancient times when instructors were few and students often traveled many miles for a once-a-week or once-a-month lesson. Forms in those days provided students with as realistic a practice method as possible, since sparring partners were virtually nonexistent. Today, although we have sparring practice to teach us timing, reaction, and strategy, we continue to practice forms for the balance, speed, form, coordination benefits.

BASIC CHARACTERISTICS

In general, forms of Okinawan origin stress low, strong stances, and powerful techniques, mostly with the hands. Most Japanese forms are originally derived from Okinawan forms, with more emphasis on speed and long, low stances. Korean forms offer many open-hand blocks and some circular motions, but their distinctive trademark is their emphasis on kicking techniques, particularly the high kicks predominately missing in the traditional Japanese and Okinawan forms. Chinese forms are characterized by the "circular" motions that dominate among the blocks and kicks, and the emphasis on open-hand strikes. American forms emphasize high hand positions and techniques that are directly applicable to free-fighting situations.

Nearly all schools and systems require that certain forms be learned for rank advancement. Most systems have from two to five forms for each new rank, although this number varies widely from system to system and instructor to instructor.

LEARNING AND MASTERING A FORM

The first step in learning a form is obviously to memorize the movements. This way prove more difficult than you might think, and the concept of *segmenting* or *sequencing* can help you impress unfamiliar moves into your memory. This concept helps overcome the difficulty of remembering more than five or six moves at a time by breaking the form into segments of fewer moves, usually three to five. It thus becomes easier to memorize five or six "segments" of five or six moves each than to try to remember thirty or more consecutive movements.

Once the moves in the form are memorized, concentrate on executing each one with perfect timing, speed, balance, and form. Use mirrors and partners (a tear-out partner-evaluation form is included at the end of this chapter) to help determine your progress.

After the movements in the form can be executed with adequate precision and effectiveness, turn your emphasis to the final goal of *vitalization.* This term means the "bringing to life" of the form: the "dramatization" that takes the form from a mere set of movements to an unfolding chronicle of combat. To do this you should attempt to block all distractions from your mind and concentrate strictly on executing all movements in both a physical and mental sense — with the feel of being involved in a real fighting situation. The impact on the form is clearly noticeable to the trained eye, and the increased training benefits of running a "vitalized" form are manifold.

BEGINNING FORMS

Although varying widely from instructor to instructor, requirements for the first belt after white usually include the knowledge of, and reasonable proficiency with, several basic forms that include fundamental techniques. The basic forms for most Japanese, Korean, Okinawan, and American styles follow what has become known as the "I-pattern" or "H-pattern" format, which is simply a description of the path followed by the student should the form be viewed from above as it progresses. (The "I" viewpoint would be as viewed facing the same direction as the starting position of the student, while the "H" viewpoint is simply turned 90 degrees — an "I" on its side.)

The first basic I-pattern form presented provides practice in the following basic techniques: the attention, ready, and front stances; the low and high forearm blocks, and the step-through front-hand straight punch. In addition, three turns are practiced — 90°, 180°, and 270°. Your instructor may use this form exactly as presented, or may alter several of the techniques before authorizing its use.

Figure 17-1 is a graphic floor plan of the first I-pattern form, showing directions of travel and numbers that correspond with the numbering of the pictures of the form being run in figure 17-2.

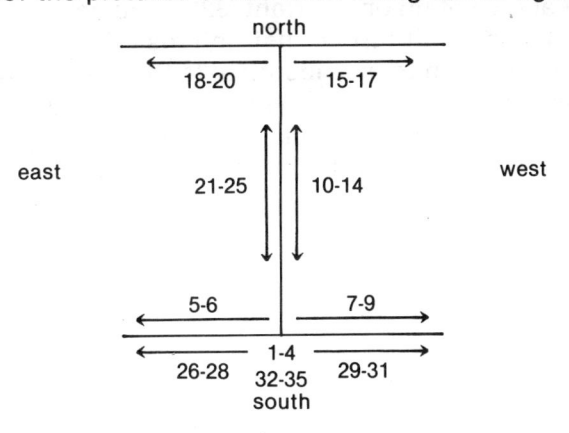

Figure 17-1 — Floor plan for first I-pattern form.

Figure 17-2 — The first I-pattern form by sequence.

The form starts from the attention stance (1). Bow (2); return to the attention stance (3); then assume the ready position (4). The first move is a step to the left ("west") and back ("south") with the left foot, simultaneous with a 90° turn into a front stance and execution of a left low forearm block against a front kick (5). Step through into another front stance with a straight punch to the midsection (6). Step back behind you and over with your front (right) foot, setting down in a spot that will provide for a good front stance upon your turn. Stay low, keeping your center of gravity down, and prepare your right hand for another low block (7). Complete the 180° turn and low forearm block. You are now in a front stance facing "east" (8). Step through with a punch (9) as in step number 6. Prepare for a 90° turn to the "north" (10), again staying low. Make your turn into another front stance with a low block (11). Procede "north" stepping three times into front stances with front-arm high forearm blocks (12, 13, 14). Prepare for a 270° turn to the "east", bringing the rear foot over and up, staying low, and preparing the left arm for a low forearm block (15). Complete the turn and block (16), and step with your straight punch to the midsection (17). Prepare for a 180° turn to the west, moving the right foot back and over (18). Complete the turn into a front stance and low block (19). Step through and punch to the midsection (20). Prepare for a 90° turn back to the "south", moving the front (left) foot back and out (21). Complete your turn and low block (22). Move through three stepping straight midsection punches from front stances (23, 24, 25). Again prepare a 270° turn as in (14), only this time you will be facing "west" after your turn (26). Make your turn and block (27). Step-through and punch (28). Prepare a 180° turn back to the "east" (29), and turn with your low block (30). Step through with the midsection punch and front stance (31). Return to the ready position by stepping back with the left foot and pivoting on the right (32). Assume attention stance (33), bow (34), and await further instructions (35).

The second I-pattern form is identical to the first in pattern, turns, and stances, but adds a front kick before all punches. It also replaces the low forearm block with middle outward forearm blocks, and the high forearm blocks with middle inward forearm blocks.

Forms 189

1. Begin in attention stance
2. Bow 
3. Return to attention stance 
4. Assume ready position 
5. Step left and block 
6. Step through and punch 
7. Prepare to turn 180° 
8. Complete turn with low block 
9. Step through and punch 
10. Prepare 90° turn to left

11. Complete turn with low block

12. Step through with high block

13. Step through with high block

14. Step through with high block

15. Prepare 270° turn

16. Complete turn with low block

17. Step through and punch

18. Prepare to turn 180°

19. Complete turn with low block

Forms 191

20. Step through and punch
21. Prepare 90° turn 
22. Complete turn with low block 
23. Step through and punch 
24. Step through and punch 
25. Step through and punch 
26. Prepare 270° turn 
27. Complete turn with low block 
28. Step through and punch

192   Forms

29. Prepare 180° turn

30. Complete turn with low block

31. Step through and punch

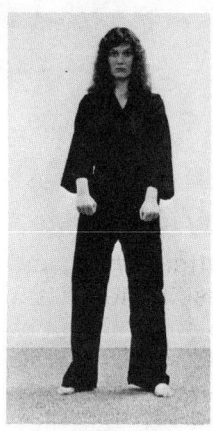

32. Return to ready stance

33. Assume attention stance

34. Bow

35. Form finishes in attention stance

Figure 17-3 — Floor plan for the second basic I-pattern form. Numbers indicate pictures of movements.

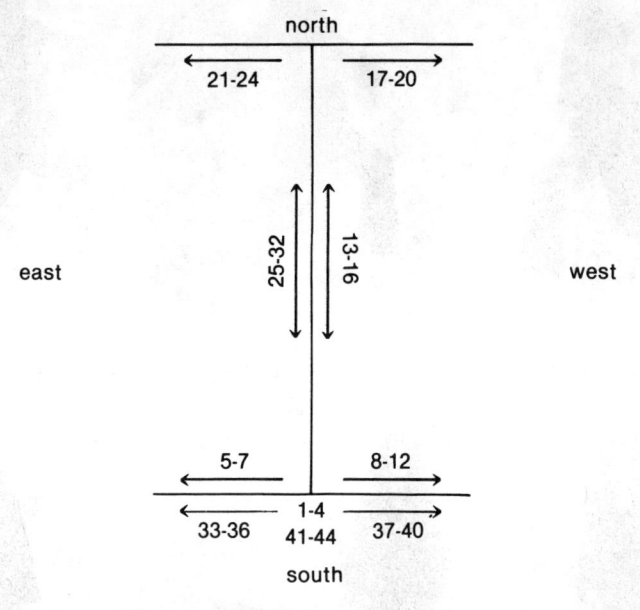

```
                        north
              ←———————   ———————→
                21-24       17-20

                         ↑ ↑
                      ଷ    ର
                      ଷ    ର
                      ଷ    ର
   east               ଷ    ର              west
                      ↓ ↓
                     25-32 13-16

                5-7         8-12
              ←—————      —————→
              ←————— 1-4  —————→
                33-36 41-44 37-40
                        south
```

Figure 17-4 — The second I-pattern form by sequence.

Begin in the attention stance (1), bow (2), return to attention (3), and assume the ready stance (4). Turn to your left ("west") into a front stance with an outward forearm block (5). Execute a rear-leg front kick, being sure to retract the leg before setting down (6) and set down into a right straight punch from a front stance (7). Prepare for your 180° turn back to the "east" (8), and turn with your outward block (9). Front kick (10) and set down again with a punch (11). Prepare for a 90° turn to the "north" (12) and turn with the outward forearm block (13). Proceed "north" through three stepping *inward* forearm blocks from front stances (14-16). Turn 270° to the "east" with the outward block (17 & 18). Execute the rear-leg front kick (19), and set down into a front stance with the straight midsection punch (20). Turn 180° back to the "west" with the outward block (21 &22) and follow with your front kick/straight punch combination (23 & 24). Turn 90° back to the "south" with the outward block (25 & 26). Proceed "south" with three front kick/straight punch combinations (27 & 28). Turn 270° to the "west" with your outward block (33 & 34), and follow with the front kick/straight punch (35 & 36). Turn 180° "east", and block with the outward block (37 & 38). Execute the front kick/straight punch combination (39 & 40). Step back with the left foot into a ready stance (41), assume attention position (42), bow (43), and return to attention to prepare for the next form or exercise (44).

194 Forms

1. Begin in attention stance
2. Bow 
3. Return to attention stance 
4. Assume ready position 
5. Step left with outward block 
6. Front kick to midsection 
7. Set down with punch 
8. Prepare for 180° turn 
9. Complete turn with outward block 
10. Front kick to midsection

Forms   195

11. Set down with punch

12. Prepare for 90° turn

13. Complete turn with outward block

14. Step through with inward forearm block

15. Step through with inward forearm block

16. Step through with inward forearm block

17. Prepare for 270° turn

18. Complete turn with outward block

19. Front kick to midsection

20. Set down with punch

21. Prepare for 180° turn

22. Complete turn with outward block

23. Front kick to midsection

24. Set down with punch

25. Prepare for 90° turn

26. Complete turn with outward block (rear view)

27. Front kick to midsection (rear view)

28. Set down with punch (rear view)

Forms 197

29. Front kick to midsection (rear view) 
30. Set down with punch (rear view) 
31. Front kick to midsection (rear view) 
32. Set down with punch (rear view)

33. Prepare to turn 270° 
34. Complete turn with outward block 
35. Front kick to midsection

36. Set down with punch
37. Prepare for 180° turn 
38. Complete turn with outward block

198 Forms

39. Front kick to midsection

40. Set down with punch

41. Return to ready position

42. Assume attention stance

43. Bow

44. Form finishes in attention stance

The so-called "single-opponent" forms are also valuable for beginners. These do not involve turns, but rather simulate a confrontation with a single opponent. The form described involves only six different techniques from beginning to end. It's real purpose however, other than to practice block/counter combinations, is to provide a format within which the student can gain experience with using different hand techniques, and how they may be incorporated into practical fighting sequences. The knifehand strike, shown in step number 9, should be replaced with a different strike and the form run again. Typically, the form is run 5-10 times consecutively, both on left and right sides, using hammerfist strikes, vertical or inverted punches, uppercuts, finger and palm-heel strikes, hook punches, jabs, or ridgehands in place of the knifehand strike.

Figure 17-5 — A single-opponent form by sequence.

Begin in the attention stance (1), bow (2), return to attention (3), and assume the ready stance (4). To perform this form on the *right* side, step back into a front stance with the right foot, and block the imaginary opponent's overhead attack with a left high forearm block (5). *(Note* — to perform this form on the left side, simply step back with the *left* foot, block with the *right* arm, and perform the remainder of the form as a mirror-image to that described.) Follow with a backfist strike with the blocking arm, attacking the bridge of the opponent's nose (6). Continue the attack with a rear-leg front kick (7), and set down forward into another front stance while executing a hand strike with the front arm (8). Double straight punches follow (9 & 10), then step back into a front stance with a low-block (11). Return to ready position (12), repeat the bowing procedure (13-15), and assume the ready position in preparation for repeating the form with a different hand technique inserted into step number 9. These could be a hammerfist strike (16), a vertical punch (17), a palm heel strike (18), one-finger strike (19), two-finger strike (20), or a ridgehand strike (21).

Remember to practice these forms at least several times a week. Pay close attention to proper form, and don't try to execute these forms too fast too soon. Proper form in your technique is more important right now than speed.

After you have become proficient in these basic forms, your instructor will allow you to go to new, intermediate-level forms, utilizing more difficult techniques and body movements.

1. Assume attention stance

2. Bow

3. Return to attention stance

4. Assume ready position

5. Step back right foot, block high

6. Backfist counterstrike

7. Front kick to midsection

8. Set down with knife-hand strike

9. Left punch middle

10. Right punch middle

11. Step back right foot, block low

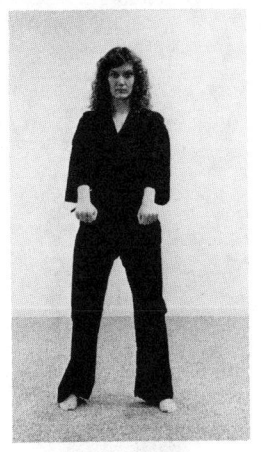

12. Return to ready stance

13. Assume attention stance

14. Bow

15. Form ends in attention stance

16. Substituting hammerfist for knifehand

17. Substituting vertical punch for knifehand

18. Substituting palm-heel strike for knifehand

19. Substituting one-finger strike for knifehand

20. Substituting two-finger strike for knifehand

21. Substituting ridgehand for knifehand

FORMS EVALUATION LIST

Tear out this page to record data when you practice to help monitor your progress. Select a training partner to evaluate your forms scoring a rating of 1 to 10 next to each evaluation criteria under each date of evaluation.

Evaluation Dates

FORM/(date learned)								
I-Pattern Form #1								
memorization								
segmenting								
balance								
speed								
form								
hand/foot timing								
effectiveness								
vitalization								
I-Pattern Form #2								
memorization								
segmenting								
balance								
speed								
form								

Dates (Continued)

hand/foot timing								
effectiveness								
vitalization								
Single-Opponent Forms								
memorization								
segmenting								
balance								
speed								
form								
hand/foot timing								
effectiveness								
vitalization								

Chapter 18
Karate for Self-Defense

BASIC PHILOSOPHY

The use of karate for self-defense involves the knowledge and application of specific target areas and techniques. The techniques used must be those (and only those!) which afford a high potential benefit with minimal risk. These techniques include well-aimed hand techniques directed at vital target areas, knee and elbow strikes, and low kicks aimed at the groin, knees, or abdomen. These techniques have a *low risk-benefit ratio.* High kicks and punches designed for "knockout," rather than structural injury, are much more risky. High kicks cause the balance to be displaced and the groin is exposed to counterattack. Knockout punches, contrary to what we see in most karate movies, are not so easy. These techniques have a *high risk-benefit ratio.* They may be highly desirable for sport karate competition, when fighting other martial artists often requires fancier techniques and the more dangerous techniques are disallowed. They do not, however, have a place in serious self-defense encounters where any risks taken may carry very high stakes.

Just knowing which techniques to use and which targets to attack is not enough. Both *physical* and *mental* preparation must occur in order for any response to an attack to be effective. Also, prepare yourself for any encounter that is contrary to your basic sense of "fair play." Self-defense is not "sporting" in any sense of the word. You must disregard any thought for the opponent's safety — a direct contrast to the attitude taken during partner work and freesparring in your class. Striking without total commitment to incapacitating the attacker will only compromise your own safety and enable your assailant to benefit from a sense of ethics that is reasonable but inappropriate under the circumstances.

PREPARING YOURSELF

The physical preparation for self-defense involves two basic stages: (1) achieving the conditioning and skill work to enable you to survive an attack and execute effective counterstrike measures and (2) practicing, with partners, the possible attacks you will face and the counterattacks you will carry out.

The conditioning work included in this book will help develop the strength, flexibility, speed, and accuracy to carry out numerous effective self-defense techniques. The partner work presented later in this chapter will give you an idea of how to practice against specific attacks, applying both physical skill and the strategic principles involved in planning a counterattack with proper timing, execution, and choice of response.

As important as physical preparation for attack is, the mental preparation is even more important. (By increasing your level of awareness with a basic understanding of the attacker, the attacker's method of operation and how you can minimize the chances of a confrontation are better understood.) Be alert at all times for trouble. Even in calm surroundings, or a place you "know is safe," unexpected emergencies may arise. You don't need to be melodramatic or conspicuous — just prepared. When walking alone, particularly at night, don't walk to a line of dark doorways or parked cars. Always allow yourself a "reaction space." In unfamiliar indoor surroundings, avoid being far from a door or other escape route. If possible, position yourself with a wall behind you. When speaking to strangers, avoid getting too close to them or between them if there are more than one. If a suspicious character asks you the time, don't lower your eyes; just hold up your watch. Avoid flashing cash in public or wearing excessive expensive jewelry. Avoid keeping your wallet in an unbuttoned back pants pocket while in a crowd, or slinging a purse over your shoulder without holding onto the strap. The less sure an attacker is that you are a worthy target or an easy target, the less likely the attacker will take a chance on you. These points may sound melodramatic, but they are realistic. Remember, taking chances could make you a loser. Your training and preparation will get you nothing if you are taken by surprise.

Once you have prepared yourself as best you can to avoid an encounter, prepare yourself mentally to handle any encounters you cannot *avoid*. The human nervous system regards vividly imagined experiences as "actual" experiences. Take a few minutes regularly, or before entering potentially dangerous situations, to visualize possible attacks and how you would handle them. By utilizing this "mental review," you will gain both psychological preparedness and mental "lock-in" on the physical responses your mind will be directing if they are needed. You will be much less likely to panic, and much more likely to react instinctively and effectively.

HANDLING AN ATTACK

Confrontations come in all shapes and sizes, from the simple purse-snatching to armed robbery. It may be a fistfight over a car accident or street-gang assault. Whatever the circumstances, remember these important principles:

1. **Don't be dangerously defensive.** Reasoning with a troublemaker or "talking your way out of it" are usually preferable to an actual confrontation. Sometimes you can just walk away, for you really have nothing to prove. However, your attacker does not always cooperate with this, so you must recognize this reality before it works against you. Never turn your back on an attacker, and *never* assume the attacker will refrain from any level of violence because of compassion, reason, or because you are smaller. Most attackers like nothing better than to prey on those who are intimidated, scared, have a false sense of security, or appear physically unable to defend themselves. Avoid, in particular, offering any bluffs or threats, which are ploys of the desperate and frightened. Any experienced attacker will know this instinctively.

Also, do not give any indication of your abilities. Forewarning is only forearming. The chances it will "scare him off" are slim, indeed, as it is confidence in his own abilities that encourages his attack in the first place. Better to let him be the one with the false sense of security. Keep surprise on your side. In addition, he could take your warning as a challenge, no matter how humbly you voice it, and it could help push a verbal encounter over the edge into violence.

In reality, once an opponent is committed to violence, the time for words has passed. There is really nothing to be said to an attacker, other than perhaps a simple "I don't want any trouble" or "you're making a mistake" before the action begins.

When you know an attack is imminent, **don't wait to absorb the first strike.** Attack the attacker! A good offense is many times the best defense, and there is nothing ethical about taking punishment you know is coming before you give out some of your own. Don't allow the attacker to benefit from a mistaken sense of morality. You will usually know instinctively when he has decided on violence, and nearly all state assault laws say that you need only be in reasonable fear for your well-being before launching your own attack. Don't take chances by waiting!

2. **Expect to take punishment.** No matter who you are, what you know, or how prepared you believe yourself to be, expect to absorb some punishment during an attack. The idea of training is not to allow you to emerge unscathed from any confrontation, but to minimize the extent and severity of possible injury while preventing further attack. Protect vital areas such as spine, neck and throat, head, chest, and groin. Blows taken on the shoulders, arms, or thighs are usually not incapacitating unless a weapon is involved (see below on weapons attacks). The best thing you can do to prevent serious injury to yourself is to be aware (don't be taken by surprise); keep your body conditioned, your defensive skills honed and reflexes sharp, and strike back quickly and decisively. You must be effective enough defensively to avoid taking an incapacitating first strike, either by blocking or avoiding, and effective enough offensively to either incapacitate the attacker or cause the attacker to break off the attack.

3. **Stress simplicity and effectiveness in your counterattacks.** "Low risk-benefit techniques" are the ones you should use — a lot of potential benefit for you with little risk. Attack eyes, throat, groin, and knee joints as primary targets, using fingers, punches, knifehands, or other hand techniques along with low kicks. Round and side kicks to the knee are very effective. Don't attempt to "spar" with an opponent or to attack less vital areas. Avoid employing complicated combinations, holds, or grappling techniques; unless you are exceptionally strong and well-versed in them, they will probably fail you. And definitely do **not** attempt to match strength with an attacker who may be much stronger than he appears. If he grabs you, don't think of making him let go — rather, make him *want* to let go. Areas such as the eyes and groin are no stronger on one person than another. Also, avoid going to the ground with an assailant. You lose many of the advantages your training has given you, as well as removing any chance of immediate mobile escape. You are in big trouble if you're on the ground and a second attacker shows up. If you do go down, regain your feet as quickly as possible while executing what techniques you can from the ground.

Above all, **do not underestimate the attacker.** Muggers and trouble makers rarely possess anything resembling genuine combative skill, but often they are quite tough, and they are always experienced. However, this same experience will also tell your assailant there are easier prey than those who strike back quickly and ruthlessly with simple, direct, effective techniques. Also, be sure to follow-up your counterattack! If you stun an attacker with your initial counterstrike, follow immediately with an incapacitating technique. He may recover almost instantly, and failing to follow-up means you will only have to do, or try to do, the job again once he regains his senses. Finally, once he is hurt badly enough so he cannot follow, utilize escape routes immediately.

4. **Attacks by an armed opponent are very different from attacks by unarmed opponents.** It is beyond the scope of this book to extensively review attacks by opponents brandishing weapons. The techniques used, reflexes required, and speed and accuracy of movement are usually advanced beyond the beginner level. However, this does not mean that you cannot use what you know effectively against certain weapon attacks, particularly club or knife attacks. It *will* take specific practice of responses for those attacks, and a higher level of confidence to accomplish them. Just remember two extremely important principles: protect vital areas at all costs and control the weapon as soon as possible.

Different weapons also present different problems. Knives and clubs are dangerous only when the opponent is relatively close to you. It also takes some amount of skill on the part of the attacker to employ them effectively. If your skill, speed, and relexes are better than his you should win; if they aren't, you lose. With weapons, that's bad, but at least you have a chance if your skills are good. Against a gun, everything changes. It takes little skill to pull a trigger, and the bullet's speed is independent of the attacker's. If the attacker is out of your reach, he can still shoot you before you can reach him. For this reason, defenses against guns are reserved for the more advanced karate students, and actually involve manipulating the attacker into a position more suitable for defense and counterattack.

One final word on weapons: whether your attacker has one or not, don't think that you can't use one! During an attack, anything you have or can pick up that can be used as a weapon — sticks, pipe, rocks — should be used. Again, remember that self-defense has no rules. Fight dirty — survival is the name of the game.

EXAMPLES OF COMMON ATTACKS AND APPROPRIATE RESPONSES

Punching attacks

Most assailants will attempt punches rather than kicks, since it is unlikely that they would be trained martial artists. They will feel most comfortable using their hands, so that is what you should expect to see. Also expect a right-handed attacker to lead with a right-handed punch, and vice versa for left-handers. The punch will probably be directed to the head, and could be either a front or rear hand strike.

Figures 18-1 through 18-4 show a defense against the front-hand attack. The attacker's punch is deflected inward and downward with an inward open-hand block (figure 18-1). A side elbow strike to the chin follows the block (figure 18-2). As the attacker doubles up, a front kick using the point of the shoe is delivered to the attacker's face (figure 18-4).

Figure 18.1

Figure 18.2

Figure 18.3

Figure 18.4

Self Defense 211

In the second sequence of photos, the attack is a hooking punch delivered with the rear hand. The block is a stopping block using the palm-heel (figure 18-6 and 18-7 in close-up). Notice that the defender steps *forward* with the foot on the blocking side, thereby stopping the punch before it builds too much momentum. Notice in figure 18-8 how the attacker's punching arm is *controlled* while the elbow counterstrike is delivered. In figure 18-9, the defender's right hand has reached up and around the back of the attacker's head and pulled the head down into her knee to finish off the assailant.

Figure 18.5

Figure 18.6

Figure 18.7

Figure 18.8

Figure 18.9

212   Self Defense

Figures 18-10 through 18-14 illustrate a defense against a straight punch delivered with the rear hand. The punch is deflected down and in with a rear hand open-hand block (figure 18-11), and a downward elbow strike is used to incapacitate that arm (figure 18-12). The attacker is then taken off his feet with a front-leg sweep helped by a left-handed pull against the head (figures 18-13). The follow-up used here against the downed attacker is a stomping kick (figure 18-14).

Figure 18.10

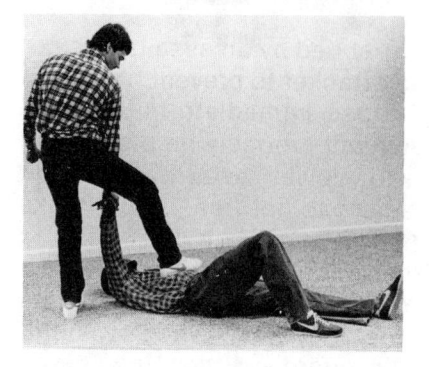

Figure 18.11

Figure 18.12

Figure 18.13

Figure 18.14

Figure 18.15

Figure 18.16

Figure 18.17

Figure 18.18

An alternate defense against the straight rear-hand punch is shown in figures 18-15 through 18-18. The defender *sidesteps* the punch and, rather than blocking, counters with a punch of his own (figure 18-16). He follows-up with a roundhouse kick to the midsection (figure 18-17) and a knifehand strike to the back of the neck (figure 18-18). (NOTE: Remember, strikes to the back of the neck can cause serious injury, including quadraplegia or even death, and should only be used in genuinely *serious* self-defense encounters.)

Grabbing attacks

The main thing to remember when grabbed by an assailant is not to panic. A grab is usually used by an attacker to prevent his victim from running away, rather than to cause immediate injury. Also remember that anyone who grabs you will probably be bigger and stronger than you, therefore don't try to "power" away from him. Instead, use leverage or angular movement to get free, or just make your attacker *want* to let go, by causing him enough discomfort to want to change his position. In either case, don't think that your move has to be made immediately. Your attacker probably expects some resistance and expects it to come right away. When you don't immediately resist, he may lower his guard a little. Unless you

214 Self Defense

believe other attackers are on the way, don't be afraid to wait a few seconds, or even longer, before acting. You'll get your chance.

Figures 18-19 through 18-23 illustrate an excellent defense against a two-handed throat grab from the front. The attacker may be trying to choke the victim, but more likely he wants to frighten and hold his victim before initiating further action. The counterattack is a finger attack to both eyes (figure 18-20). This should prompt the attacker to release his grip, and protect his eyes, at least momentarily, from further injury. Before following up with the side elbow strike (figure 18-21 and 18-22), be sure the opponent is distracted enough by his eye injury not to try another grab when the distance is closed. If he is not distracted, try to make an escape immediately. If he is distracted, following-up with the elbow strike and the side kick to the knee shown in figure 18-23 should help guarantee a safe escape.

Figure 18.19

Figure 18.20

Figure 18.21

Figure 18.22

Figure 18.23

An alternate to making the attacker *want* to let go, as in the last sequence, is to actually break his grip using leverage and angular motion. In figure 18-24, the victim is again grabbed by the throat. This time, the left arm is raised (for a right-handed person), and a quick clockwise turn (figures 18-25 and 18-26) will break the attacker's grip, while leading perfectly into a spinning elbow strike to the head (figures 18-27 and 18-28). Most males instinctively watch for attacks to the groin, but once the attacker's attention is distracted by the head injury, the groin becomes an excellent target for a front-leg roundhouse kick (figure 18-29).

Figure 18.24

Figure 18.25

Figure 18.26

Figure 18.27

Figure 18.28

Figure 18.29

216 Self Defense

Attacks from the rear may be startling, but if you keep your cool, you can extract yourself from them as effectively as from frontal attacks. In these rear attacks, the attacker probably just wants to immobilize the victim, at least for the moment. If he only wanted to inflict injury, his initial move would probably have been a strike rather than a grab.

The defense is one of initial relaxation, lulling the attacker into a sense of some security. Once the attacker's face is located, (either by his breathing or his voice), he can be both startled and stunned by the defender slamming the back of the head into the soft tissue of his face and nose (figure 18-31). Again, this will draw his attention away from his groin, which can then be attacked by shifting the hip to one side and using a knifehand strike (figure 18-32). If the attacker still hasn't let go, head slams and groin strikes are continued until he does. Once he does let go, a back kick to the groin is a good finishing move as the intended victim begins to sprint from the scene (figure 18-33).

Figure 18.30

Figure 18.31

Figure 18.32

Figure 18.33

Self Defense 217

Figure 18.34

Figure 18.35

Figure 18.36

Figure 18.37

Figure 18.38

A wrist grab is extremely easy to break. Again, relax a little, and so will he. Then, moving very quickly and forefully, pull the arm away *in the direction that opposes the thumb* (figures 18-34 and 18-35). An immediate strike to your attacker's temple with a hammerfist strike (figure 18-36), followed by a reverse punch to the throat (figure 18-37) and a groin kick (figure 18-38), serve to incapacitate the attacker.

Weapon attacks

In all weapon attacks, again assume that the attacker will be handling the weapon with his strong arm (i.e., a right hander will use his right arm). Your goals are, in order of importance and occurrence: (a) to keep from being injured by his initial attack (b) to control the weapon and prevent a second strike with it against you, and (c) to follow-up with your own counterstrike to incapacitate the attacker and end the confrontation.

The first attacker shown is planning an overhand strike using a ball bat or club. As the attack is blocked with a high block (figure 18-40), step to the *outside* of the attacker's front foot, keeping the non-blocking hand held high to protect against punches thrown with this free hand (note that *the step must be forward* to enable you to block his arm and not the club!). Once the attacker's club arm is controlled with the blocking arm, a palm heel strike to the chin simultaneous with a front foot sweep (figure 18-41) immobilizes the attacker. Any appropriate follow-up will do, including the punch shown in figure 18-42.

Figure 18.39

Figure 18.40

Figure 18.41

Figure 18.42

In all attacks involving knives, be very aware of critical distance. Your attacker must be much closer to cut you with a knife than to hit you with a club, but once in range, he can do a lot of damage fast. Grasp his knife hand quickly and don't let go until he drops the knife! Also, expect that you may get cut. Cuts taken on the forearms, shoulders, thighs, or midsection are not nearly as bad as those on the wrists, hands, neck, or face. Avoid straight-in (stab) attacks directed to the midsection, chest, throat, or face. Protect these areas at all costs until you can disarm your attacker, or get away.

Figures 18-43 through 18-52 depict a straight-in stabbing attack to the chest or midsection. The intended victim sidesteps the strike while deflecting and grabbing the attacker's wrist (figures 18-44 and 18-45 in close-up). The other hand is added (figure 18-46) as the

Figure 18.43

Figure 18.44

Figure 18.45

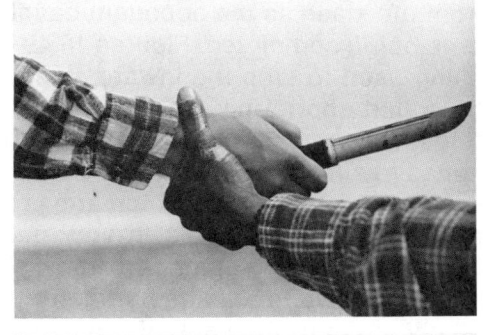

Figure 18.46

Figure 18.47

Figure 18.48

defender continues moving clockwise, pivoting on the forward foot (figure 18-47). As a position is reached with the back to the opponent's side (and therefore not easily reachable with his free hand), a downward pull on the attacker's arm combined with a push-up with the legs from a side stance (figure 18-48), cause pressure on his elbow joint. This should result in the attacker dropping the knife as well as injuring the elbow joint and preventing further attack.

Against a slashing attack, your priority is to either back away from the slash so the opponent cannot reach you, or stop the slash from being completed. Figures 18-49 - 18-50 show a knifehand block being used to stop the inward slash (notice that, should the slash be pulled short, only the side of the blocking hand would be cut. *Under no circumstances* should the hand be turned in such a manner as to allow the knife to cut the back of the hand, or inside of the wrist or fingers). The slashing arm is not only immediately grabbed, but the defender moves in very quickly, jamming any future attempts at slashing again. An elbow strike stuns the attacker (figure 18-51), followed by a knee strike to the groin (figure 18-52), and an elbow strike to the back of the neck (figure 18-53).

The self-defense examples shown are included not to teach the "proper" response to a particular attack but rather to give you an idea of the *principles you must understand and utilize* to come up with your own effective responses to any number of different kinds of attacks. Only with constant mental review and physical practice can you be sure that defenses you design will be effective in an actual encounter.

Self Defense 221

Figure 18.49

Figure 18.50

Figure 18.51

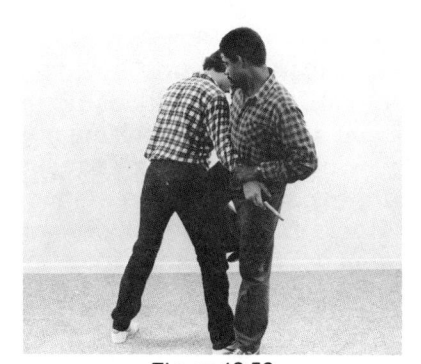

Figure 18.52

Figure 18.53

EXERCISE

As an exercise to develop and test your understanding of basic self-defense principles, plan your own step-by-step responses to the attacks detailed below (try to be original, although you may use techniques already shown you in this chapter):

1. ATTACK: Straight punch delivered to the face with the front hand.

   RESPONSE: _____
   _____
   _____
   _____
   _____

2. ATTACK: Reverse punch to the mid-section.

   RESPONSE: _____
   _____
   _____
   _____
   _____

3. ATTACK: Kick to the groin.

   RESPONSE: _____
   _____
   _____
   _____

4. ATTACK: One-handed grab to the throat from the front.

   RESPONSE: _____
   _____
   _____
   _____

5. ATTACK: Two-handed grab of the upper arms, from the front.

   RESPONSE: _____
   _____
   _____
   _____

6. ATTACK: Two-handed grab around the neck, from the back.
   RESPONSE: _____
   _____
   _____
   _____

7. ATTACK: One-arm grab around the throat, from the back.
   RESPONSE: _____
   _____
   _____
   _____

8. ATTACK: One-armed headlock, facing same direction.
   RESPONSE: _____
   _____
   _____
   _____

9. ATTACK: Baseball bat, swung from side to side, body level.
   RESPONSE: _____
   _____
   _____
   _____

10. ATTACK: Downward stabbing knife attack, from front.
    RESPONSE: _____
    _____
    _____
    _____

CHAPTER 18 EVALUATION

Multiple Choice: Circle the letter of the correct answer.
1. Effective self-defense requires the use of techniques affording high benefit with little potential risk. We call these techniques:
   a. elbow and knee strikes
   b. low risk-benefit ratio techniques
   c. roundhouse or side-kick strikes
   d. high risk-benefit ratio techniques
2. Physical preparation for self-defense involves which two stages?
   a. conditioning and skill work followed by partner practice
   b. partner practice followed by mental review
   c. mental review followed by partner practice
   d. conditioning and skill work followed by mental review
3. Two very important principles to remember during weapons attacks are:
   a. attack the attacker, and different weapons present different problems
   b. risk-benefit ratio and practice on specifics
   c. protect vital areas and mental review
   d. protect vital areas and control the weapon as soon as possible

Fill in the blanks:
1. High kicks or knockout punches would be examples of _____ risk-benefit ratio techniques. Knee or elbow strikes would be examples of _____ risk-benefit ratio techniques.

2. The preparation for effective self-defense must take into account both the physical and the _____.

3. A wrist grab may easily be broken by pulling the arm away in a direction that *opposes* the attacker's _____.

Chapter 19
Karate for Sport

Although originally developed as an art of self-defense, karate is also well suited for adaptation as a sport. When conducted under the proper rules, competition karate is safe, fun, and can provide a valuable learning experience for male and female students of all ages and ranks.

HISTORY

Controlled contests between karate practitioners first became popular in the Orient during the mid-150s, with National Championships being held in Korea in 1953 and Japan in 1957. The first karate tournament held in the United States was probably Robert Trias' Arizona Karate Championships, held in Phoenix in 1955. By the early 1960s, attempts were being made to host National U.S. championships, most notably Jhoon Rhee's 1st U.S. National Karate Championships, held in Washington D.C., in 1964, and Ed Parker's 1st International Karate Championships, also held in 1964, in Long Beach, California.

In 1968, New Yorker promoter Aaron Banks held the first American version of the World Karate Championships, and the four World Titles were all won by Americans: *Joe Lewis* (heavyweight), *Mike Stone* (light heavyweight), *Chuck Norris* (middleweight), and *Skipper Mullins* (lightweight). This competition was of a non-contact variety, with no protective equipment worn by the contestants. Banks discontinued the event several years later.

In 1970, the World Union of Karate-do Organizations (WUKO) held its version of the World Championships in Tokyo. The WUKO remains the primary sanctioning body for the non-contact version of karate competition, and annually holds its World Championships with many member countries represented.

In 1972, Jhoon Rhee, a Korean-born martial artist with several successful karate schools in the Washington D.C. area, invented the first crude items of karate safety equipment. Although ugly and bulky, the foam rubber gloves and boots drastically reduced accidental injuries during sparring and forever changed the face of American competitive karate.

In 1973, the first karate tournament allowing light contact with safety gloves and boots was held in St. Louis. From then until the present, nearly all major U.S. Open karate competitions allow light contact to be made and require the use of safety equipment among the participants. Most tournaments in the Orient and Europe remain non-contact events with safety equipment disallowed, but these areas also are adopting light-contact and mandatory safety equipment rules to a greater degree every year.

In 1974, the Professional Karate Association, the original sanctioning body for full-contact karate, was founded and held its first World Championships in Los Angeles. Using the foam rubber safety equipment, the participants, including representatives from the U.S., Japan, Mexico, Germany, Canada, and other countries, fought without any restrictions on contact; although the more dangerous techniques, such as elbows and knees, were disallowed and certain vital target areas were off limits. Although some matches ended in knockouts, none of the participants were seriously injured, and the forerunner of the contact karate we see now on television was born. *Isaias Duenas* (Mexico), *Bill Wallace* (U.S.) *Jeff Smith* (U.S.) and *Joe Lewis* (U.S.) all won world titles at the event.

The late 1970s and early '80s saw competition karate beginning to grow in all areas. Martial artists began taking a new interest in *forms* competition, previously thought of as primarily for "non-fighters." Elaborate forms, developed strictly for competition, became the mainstay of the top competitors. Non-contact karate, still will bare hands and feet, lost popularity in the U.S. but thrived in foreign countries. Light-contact "point" karate flourished throughout America, helped to a great degree by the emergence of widely-traveling talented national superstars such as Keith Vitali and Raymond McCallum, and an organized circuit of major events. Full-contact karate emerged as a premier spectator event and in 1976 began attracting coverage by the major television networks.

Today, due to the efforts of the prominent sanctioning bodies and *Karate Illustrated* magazine, point tournaments in the United States have organized into circuits of C,B,A, and AA events. The AA circuit consists of the prime national events, and currently includes the Battle of Atlanta, the West Coast Nationals (San Jose), the Diamond Nationals (Minneapolis), the LAMA Nationals (Chicago), and the U.S. Open (Florida). Full-contact karate events are held in nearly every state and major city in the U.S., and are a regular feature on several television networks.

TYPES OF COMPETITION

Forms

Forms competition is included at nearly all tournaments today, with the exception of full-contact events. At a typical 400-competitor tournament, nearly 200 competitors will compete in forms.

The object of forms competition is to present a form which will show your talents and impress the judges. Three to seven judges, all black belts, watch the form and give each contestant a score, usually based on a 0.0 - 10.0 decimal system. For under-black belts, scores typically average around 6.0, with 7.0 to 7.5 being an excellent score. Black belts generally are scored higher, with about 7.0 being the average and 8.0 to 8.5 being a high score. Top nationally-ranked black belts often score in the 9.5 - 9.9 range during championship competition. A square "ring" 20 feet by 20 feet is marked off on the floor, usually with tape. The floor is typically made of wood, concrete, or a rubberized surface. The five dark "belted" circles in figure 19-1 represent the black belt judges, while the light "belted" circles represent the contestants. The circles marked with an X are scorekeepers. (An alternate set-up has the judges placed in each corner, with the Center Judge remaining at the top of the ring). The circle within the square has had his or her name called by the scorekeeper, and is preparing to run his or her form. After the form is run, the contestant will remain stationary while the judges, upon the command of the designated Center Judge, (usually the highest ranking black belt or the judge with the most experience), simultaneously announce their score to the

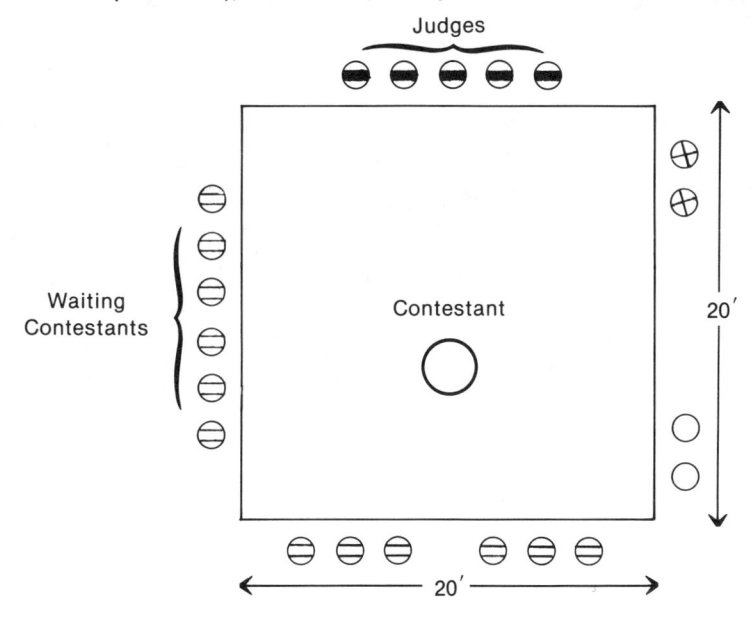

230   **Karate for Sport**

score-keeper using cards with decimal numbers on them. Forms are scored on the criteria of speed, power, balance, grace, vitalization, difficulty factor, and overall effectiveness. If more than three judges are used, the high and low scores are usually dropped and the other scores added to determine that contestant's score. After being scored, the contestant takes his or her place back outside the ring, and the next form is run.

Table 19-1 lists the divisions which are typical for forms competition.

Notice that, in addition to empty-handed forms, forms using Oriental weapons are also run, and have separate divisions or black belts and under-black belts. Figure 19-2 shows a form using a Japanese staff, or *bo*.

Figure 19.2, Weapons competition using the staff, or *bo*.

Figure 19.3, Women's empty-handed forms competition.

Karate for Sport 231

Figure 19.4, Men's empty-handed forms competition, featuring John Chung, two-time National Forms Champion.

Figure 19.5, Awards ceremony after men's forms competition.

Figure 19.6, 1980 U.S. Open, a major national tournament, just prior to the start of forms competition. Notice the taped and numbered rings spread across the floor for the individual rank competitions. Many of the judges and competitors are already in place.

For a detailed account of rules for forms competition, see Appendix F.

Fighting

Among open style American tournaments, **light-contact** tournaments are much more popular than non-contact tournaments. Safety equipment of the type shown in figure 19-7 is required of all contestants. Mouthguards are also required or highly recommended, and groin protectors are required for males. Shin guards are optional.

Non-contact tournaments have diminished greatly in popularity since the advent of safety equipment in 1972. However, some competitions are still held. Contestants are not permitted to wear any safety equipment other than a mouthguard, groin protector, and shin guards. All techniques are supposed to be stopped short of actual face contact (light contact to the *body* is allowed), but quite often contact is made. When this happens, the offender is either warned, penalized a point, or disqualified, depending on the severity and intent of the infraction.

Karate for Sport

Figure 19.7, Men's light-contact fighting competition.

Figure 19.8, Fighting competitor wearing the mandatory foam rubber hand and foot gear. Notice the mouthpiece stuck behind the belt for safekeeping between matches.

The arrangement for competition in non-contact or light-contact is as shown below:

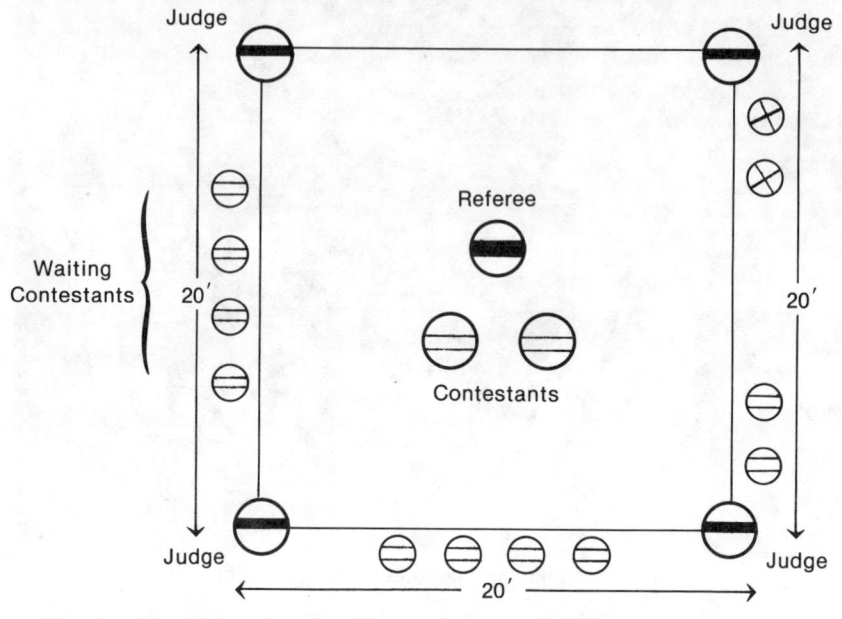

Again, the black "belted" circles are the judges, and the white "belted" circles are the contestants. Two contestants are shown in the ring preparing to begin their bout. The judge within the ring is known as the "Referee" and serves to start and stop the contest, as well as vote. The Referee also penalizes the contestants if necessary.

Typically, matches last for 2 or 3 minutes. The fighter scoring the most points within that time limit is declared the winner, or often the rules state that the first fighter to reach three points is the winner. In non-contact matches, this is often altered to a *half-point* and *full-point* system. Most scoring techniques would garner the fighter only one-half point. Two half-points, or one perfect strike, with the potential to disable if carried through, to win the match for a fighter.

After the Referee begins the match, the contestants attempt to score on one another while free-sparring. If any judge sees a scoring technique, he or she shouts "point!" and the Referee commands the fighters to "stop!" They return to the center of the ring, and wait motionless while the judges vote on who, if anyone, they believed scored, based on a raise of flags. (One fighter is designated the "red" fighter, and the other the "white" fighter.) A majority of the judges' votes is required to award a point (either three or five judges are always used). The judges look for techniques that are fast, strong and clearly landed but not focused so

Karate for Sport 235

Figure 19.9, Men's light-contact fighting competition.

Figure 19.10, Women's light-contact fighting competition.

deep as to cause injury. Certain dangerous techniques, such as finger jabs and knee and elbow strikes, are not allowed, and certain target areas such as the spine, throat, back of neck, and groin are off limits as targets. (Some tournaments allow groin as a no-contact target in the adult or adult brown and black belt divisions only.)

Contestants may also be *penalized* for such infractions as striking with too much contact, using an illegal technique, attacking an illegal target area, leaving the ring boundary to avoid attack, showing disrespect to a judge, etc.

Table 19-2 lists divisions commonly used for light-contact tournaments.

For a detailed listing of rules and conduct of bouts, see Light-Contact Rules in Appendix D.

Since its inception in the mid 1970s, **full-contact** karate has grown rapidly. Competitions are now held inside regulation boxing-type rings, and boxing gloves or specially made leather karate gloves are used, along with the foam rubber foot pads. Rounds are two minutes each and the length of matches follows the schedule below:

Amateur non-title bouts - 3 or 4 rounds
Amateur State, Regional, or National Title bouts - 5 rounds
Professional non-title bouts - 5, 6, 7, 8, 9, 10 or 11 rounds
Professional State Title bouts - 7 rounds
Professional Regional Title bouts - 8 rounds
Professional National Title bouts - 9 rounds
Professional World Title bouts - 12 rounds

Figure 19.11, Undefeated former PKA World Middleweight Champion Bill "Superfoot" Wallace in a 1980 full-contact title defense.

Figure 19.12, PKA World Featherweight Champion Jerry Clarke (right) in a full-contact bout against World Bantamweight Champion Felipe Garcia.

Full-contact fighters follow a very rigorous training schedule — far tougher than the average karate student. Running, bagwork, sparring, and body-conditioning calisthenics are vital to the full-contact fighter's training regimen. Most fighters are 18-28 years old (amateurs may be as young as 16 years), as compared to light-contact fighters who may continue tournament fighting well into their thirties. All professional full-contact fighters are black belts, while amateurs may be black belts or under-black belts.

Weight divisions have been expanded to the present number of 11 as follows:

Atomweight	under 113 lbs.
Flyweight	113-118.9 lbs.
Bantamweight	119-125.9 lbs.
Featherweight	126-132.9 lbs.
Lightweight	133-139.9 lbs.
Lightwelterweight	140-147.9 lbs.
Welterweight	148-155.9 lbs.
Lightmiddleweight	156-163.9 lbs.
Middleweight	164-171.9 lbs.
Lightheavyweight	172-179.9 lbs.
Heavyweight	180-194.9 lbs.
Superheavyweight	195 and over

(See Appendix I for past and present PKA World Full-Contact Karate Champions.)

Although some women's full-contact matches have been held, the women's divisions have yet to really become organized or see much activity. Part of the problem is the lack of development of a set of rules that would be suitable for women's competition.

A typical night of full-contact karate action includes four to six amateur bouts of 3-5 rounds in length, two to four preliminary professional fights of 5-8 rounds each, and a professional main event bout of 8-12 rounds, with a Regional, National or World Title at stake. Such programs of full-contact karate action have been shown both live and delayed on cable and network television and have drawn live gates of up to 10,000 spectators.

The diagram of a full-contact competition is shown below.

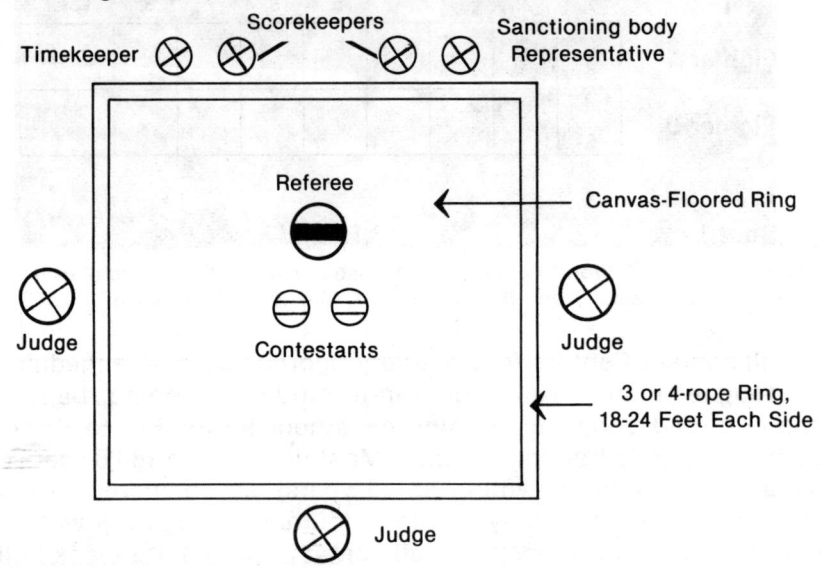

```
                    Scorekeepers
  Timekeeper    ⊗  ⊗     ⊗  ⊗    Sanctioning body
                                  Representative
  ┌──────────────────────────────────┐
  │ ┌──────────────────────────────┐ │
  │ │                              │ │
  │ │          Referee             │ │
  │ │            ⊖         ←────── │ │── Canvas-Floored Ring
  │ │                              │ │
⊗ │ │         ⊖  ⊖                 │ │ ⊗
Judge│         Contestants          │ │ Judge
  │ │                              │ │
  │ │                         ←─── │ │── 3 or 4-rope Ring,
  │ │                              │ │   18-24 Feet Each Side
  │ └──────────────────────────────┘ │
  └──────────────────────────────────┘
                   ⊗  Judge
```

Each judge scores the fight round by round, giving the winner of each round a score of 10, and the loser a score of 5-9, depending on his relative performance. The judges base their scores primarily on the *effectiveness* of the fighters — i.e., *who was able to score on the other fighter with visible effect.* Whereas light-contact rules penalize fighters for hitting too hard, full-contact rules reward it. Indeed, a knockout or technical knockout is an instant win, as in boxing. The referee starts and stops the fighters at the beginning and end of each round, and assesses any necessary penalties (clinching or holding, striking with the head, elbow, or knee, or attaching off-limits targets are penalties). Fighters are required to execute a specified minimum number of kicks per round, to prevent hands only, non-karate fighters from entering the competition.

For a detailed listing of full-contact rules and divisions, see Appendix H. A scoring sheet is provided at the end of this chapter to help you see how close you come to the official judges scores on the next televised full-contact bouts you see.

Full-Contact Scorecard

Bout 1   **Round**

	1	2	3	4	5	6	7	8	Total
Fighter A									
Fighter B									

Bout 2   **Round**

	1	2	3	4	5	6	7	8	Total
Fighter A									
Fighter B									

Bout 3   **Round**

	1	2	3	4	5	6	7	8	Total
Fighter A									
Fighter B									

Bout 4   **Round**

	1	2	3	4	5	6	7	8	Total
Fighter A									
Fighter B									

Give the winner of each round 10 points, and the loser 5-9 points, depending on his relative performance. Use *effectiveness, control of the other fighter,* and *overall ability* as criteria. Most of your scores (probably over 90%) will be 10-9. 10-8 would indicate one fighter really dominated or knocked the other fighter down. 10-7 would mean at least two knockdowns and complete domination by one fighter. 10-6 and 10-5 are almost never used. They indicate a totally one-sided fight, with at least three knockdowns in the round.

If you think a round was even, score it 10-10.

TABLE 19-1
FORM'S DIVISIONS

Event Size	Small Local Competition	Medium Statewide Competition	Large Regional Competition	Very Large National Competition
Approximate Number Competitors	Under 200	200-400	400-700	Over 700
Under-adult Divisions	8 years and under (all belts)	8 years and under (all belts)	6 years and under (all belts)	6 years and under (all belts)
Age and belt color	9 and 10 years (all belts)	9 and 10 years (all belts)	7 and 8 years (all belts)	7 and 8 years (white/green)
	11 and 12 years (all belts)	11 and 12 years (white/green)	9 and 10 years (white/green)	7 and 8 years (brown/black)
	13-15 years (white/green)	11 and 12 years (brown/black)	9 and 10 years (brown/black)	9 and 10 years (white/green)
	13-15 years (brown/black)	13-15 years (white/green)	11 and 12 years (white/green)	9 and 10 years (brown/black)
		13-15 years (brown/black)	11-12 years (brown/black)	11 and 12 years (white)
			13-15 years (white)	11 and 12 years (green)
			13-15 years (green)	11 and 12 years (brown/black)
			13-15 years (brown/black)	13-15 years (white)
				13-15 years (green)
				13-15 years (brown/black)

Adult Divisions

Sex and belt color

men and women together	men:	men:	women:
white	white	white	white
green	green	green	green
brown	brown	brown	brown
black	black	black hard style	black hard style
under black weapons		black soft style	black soft style
	women:	women:	men and women together
	white	white	under black weapons
	green	green	black weapons - hard style
	brown	brown	black weapons - soft style
	black	black	black belts over 35 years
	men and women together	black Japanese style	
	under black weapons	black Okinawan style	
	black weapons	black Korean style	
		black Chinese style	
		men and women together	
		under black weapons	
		black belts over 35 years	

TABLE 19-2
FIGHTING DIVISIONS

Event Size	Small Local Competition	Medium Statewide Competition	Large Regional Competition	Very Large National Competition
Approximate Number Competitors	Under 200	200-400	400-700	Over 700
Under-adult Divisions	8 years and under (all belts)	8 years and under (all belts)	6 years and under (all belts)	6 years and under (all belts)
	9 and 10 years (all belts)	9 and 10 years (all belts)	7 and 8 years (all belts)	7 and 8 years (white/green)
	11 and 12 years (all belts)	11 and 12 years (white/green)	9 and 10 years (white/green)	7 and 8 years (brown/black)
	13-15 years (white/green)	11 and 12 years (brown/black)	9 and 10 years (brown/black)	9 and 10 years (white/green)
	13-15 years (brown/black)	13-15 years (white/green)	11 and 12 years (white/green)	9 and 10 years (brown/black)
		13-15 years (brown/black)	11-12 years (brown/black)	11 and 12 years (white)
		13-15 years girls (all belts)	13-15 years (white)	11 and 12 years (green)
			13-15 years (green)	11 and 12 years (brown/black)
			13-15 years (brown/black)	13-15 years (white)
			13-15 years girls (all belts)	13-15 years (green)

(Continued)

	13-15 years (brown/black)	13-15 years girls (all belts)
Adult Divisions (Adult men and women never fight together)	men: white green brown black light black middle black heavy	men: white light white heavy green light green heavy brown light brown heavy black light black middle black light heavy black heavy	men: white light white middle white heavy green light green middle green heavy brown light brown middle brown heavy black super - light black light black middle black light heavy black heavy under - black over 35 years
Weights are as follows: Under-black belt men: light-under 150 middle - 150-169.9 heavy - 170 and over	women: white green brown	women: white green brown black light black heavy	women: white light white heavy green light green heavy brown light brown heavy black light black heavy
Blackbelt men: superlight - under 140 light - 140-151.9 middle - 152-165.9 light heavy - 166-183.9 heavy - 184	black	men: white light white heavy green light green heavy brown light brown heavy black super - light black light black middle black light - heavy black heavy black over 35 years	
Women black belt and under: light - under 120 heavy - over 120		women: white light white heavy green light green heavy brown light brown heavy black light black heavy	

Karate for Sport   243

CHAPTER 19 EVALUATION

Multiple Choice: Circle the letter of the correct answer.

1. Controlled competitions between karate practitioners first began appearing in the Orient in the:
   a. 1930s
   b. 1940s
   c. 1950s
   d. 1960s

2. The first karate tournament in the United States was held in:
   a. 1948
   b. 1950
   c. 1955
   d. 1957

3. Forms competition is included today at:
   a. Regional tournaments only
   b. Full-contact events only
   c. Nearly all tournaments except full-contact programs
   d. National tournaments only

4. The *number* of forms divisions would be *greater* at a State competition than at a:
   a. Regional competition
   b. National competition
   c. Local competition
   d. U.S. competition

5. The most popular type of karate tournament in America is the:
   a. light-contact
   b. no-contact
   c. forms
   d. Regional-level

Fill in the blanks:

1. The first full-contact World Championships were held in _____ at _____ _____, California.

2. Forms are scored on a _____ to _____ basis, using decimals. Under-black belt scores average _____, while black belt scores average _____.

3. Forms competitions are held in a _____ by _____ foot ring taped onto the floor, and _____ to _____ judges are typically used.

4. Light contact matches usually last for either _____ or _____ minutes. Either the fighter with the most points wins, or the fighter who reaches _____ points first.

5. Amateur full-contact karate fights last for either _____, _____, or _____ rounds, which are _____ minutes each in length.

APPENDIXES

                                                                                         Page

A   Reference Books on the Martial Arts and Conditioning 248

B   Major Karate Styles 249

C   Belt Advancement Chart 253

D   Tournament Forms and Light Contact Fighting Rules 254

E   PKA Full-Contact World Champions Past and Present 261

F   Personal Advancement Record 263

G   Major Muscles of the Body 264

APPENDIX A
Reference Books on the Martial Arts and Conditioning

Anderson, Dan. *American Freestyle Karate.* Unique Publications, Inc., Hollywood, Ca. 1980.

Burton, Benjamin. *Human Nutrition.* McGraw-Hill Book Co., New York. 1976.

Chun, Richard. *Moo Duk Kwan.* Ohara Publications, Burbank, CA. 1975.

Cooper, Kenneth. *Aerobics.* Bantam Books, Inc., New York. 1968.

Corcoran, John and Farkas, Emil. *Martial Arts — Traditions, History, People.* Gallery Book, W.H. Smith Publications, Inc., New York. 1983.

Corley, Joe. *Joe Corley Basic Self-Defense.* Vol. 1, Books 1-10. Joe Corley Enterprises, Atlanta, GA. 1983.

Darden, Ellington. *How Your Muscles Work.* Anna Publishing, Inc., Winter Park, FL. 1978.

Demura, Fumio. *Shito-Ryu Karate.* Ohara Publications, Burbank, CA. 1971.

Funakoshi, Gichin. *Karate-do — My Way of Life.* Kodansha International, Tokyo, NY, San Francisco. 1975.

Han, Bong Soo. *Hapkido.* Ohara Publications, Burbank, CA. 1974.

Kim Richard. *Weaponless Warriors.* Ohara Publications, Burbank, CA. 1974.

Kurban, Roy. *Kicking Techniques.* Ohara Publications, Burbank, CA. 1979.

Lee, Bruce. *Tao of Jeet Kune Do.* Ohara Publications, Burbank, CA. 1975.

Lee, Joo Bang. *Hwa Rang Do.* Ohara Publications, Burbank, CA. 1978.

Marchini, Ron and Fong, Leo. *Power Training in Kung-Fu & Karate.* Ohara Publications, Burbank, CA. 1974.

Morris, P.M.V. *Illustrated Guide to Karate.* Van Nostrand Reinhold Company, N.Y. 1979.

Musashi, Miyamoto. *A Book of Five Rings.* Overlook Press, Woodstock, NY. 1974.

Nagamine, Shoshin. *Essence of Okinawan Karatedo.* Charles E. Tuttle Co., Rutland, VT. 1976.

Nicol, C.W. *Moving Zen.* Quill, NY. 1975.

Oyama, Mas. *This is Karate.* Japan Publications, Inc., Tokyo. 1973.

Patterson, Cecil. *Introduction to Wado-Ryu Karate.* Ohara Publications, Burbank, CA. 1974.

Tackett, Tim. *Hsing I Kung Fu.* Ohara Publications, Burbank, CA. 1972.

Tuten, Rich, Moore, Clancy, and Knight, Virgil. *Weight-Training Everyone.* Hunter Textbooks, Inc., Winston-Salem, NC. 1982.

Urquidez, Benny. *Training and Fighting Skills.* Unique Publications, Inc., Hollywood, CA. 1981.

Vitali, Keith, and Mitchell, Kent. *Karate for Beginners.* Contemporary Books, Inc., Chicago, IL. 1983.

Wallace, Bill. *Dynamic Stretching and Kicking.* Unique Publications, Inc., Hollywood, CA. 1982.

Wallace, Bill. *Karate.* Addison. Wesley Publishing. Reading, MA. 1976.

Will, Jay. *Advanced Kenpo Karate.* Unique Publications, Los Angeles, CA. 1984.

Yamashita, Tadashi. *Shorin-Ryu Karate.* Ohara Publications, Burbank, CA. 1976.

APPENDIX B
Major Karate Styles

American. First devised in the 1960s by Joe Corley, American karate emphasizes self-defense and sport karate as suited to the American physique and attitude. Originally seen as an "outcast" style by traditionalists, American karate has grown greatly in popularity during the past two decades.

Bando. Although incorporating some Chinese influences, Bando is generally thought to be native to Burma. It's chief proponent is Dr. Maung Gyi, a U.S. resident. The style is very popular in Burma, although it's worldwide following is far behind that of other major karate styles. The style includes forms, sparring, and work with traditional weaponry.

Chito-Ryu. Japanese, founded by Tsuyoshi Chitose, based on Shorin-Ryu and Goju-Ryu. Worldwide, but largest following is in Southern Japan.

Choy-Li-Fut. Chinese, direct style descendent from the ancient Shaolin Temple methods. Emphasizes long-range hand techniques in an aggressive manner. Classed as a *southern* Chinese style.

Goju-Ryu. Okinawan, founded in the 1920's by Chojun Miyagi. Based on the old Okinawan styles of Naha-te and Tomari-te. Extremely large following in Okinawa, Japan, and worldwide. Gogen Yamaguchi is present head of the system. The name means "Hard and Soft", emphasizing strong strikes and redirectional blocks.

Hapkido. Korean, one of the major karate arts of that country, along with Tae Kwon Do, Tang Soo Do, and Hwarang-Do. Founded by Yong Shul Choi in 1940, Hapkido blends the kicking techniques of Tae Kwon Do and Hwarang-Do with the restraining moves of aikido. Hapkido enjoys a moderate following in it's country of origin and in the U.S.

Hsing-I. Chinese, literally the "mind-form" style. Originated in the San-Shih province, now popular world-wide.

Hwarang-Do. Korean, an extremely complex system devised nearly two thousand years ago by the Buddhist priest Won Kwang Bopsa. For centuries, Korean warriors were taught Hwarang-Do as part of their standard military training. The style is now headquarters in California under Joo Bang Lee, and has a moderate following mainly on the west coast.

Isshin-Ryu. Okinawan, founded in 1954, by Tatsuo Shimabuku. The name means "One-Heart Style." Based on Shorin-Ryu and Goju-Ryu. Moderate popularity in Okinawa, but one of the best-known Okinawan styles in America.

Jeet Kune Do. Chinese-based, although devised from a variety of styles and cannot really be said to originate from any distinct system or pattern of fighting philosophy. The famous martial arts practitioner Bruce Lee developed Jeet Kune Do in 1967, intending for the style to not only incorporate his original Chinese learnings and contemporary techniques, but also to allow each follower of the style to express his or her own developments without being limited by style parameters. After Lee's death in 1973, teachings of the style, which means "ways of the intercepting fist," continued under the directorship of Lee's top student, Dan Inosanto. The following of this style is moderate in the U.S. (mainly California) and Europe.

Kajukenbo. Hawaiian, developed in 1947 by Adriano Emperado, who combined elements of karate, judo, jujutsu, kenpo, and boxing. The first two letters of each art became the basis for the name. Moderate following in the Hawaiian Islands and the western United States.

Kempo. A style popular in Japan, based on Chinese Shaolin kung-fu methods.

Kenpo. Often confused with Kempo. A Japanese system based on ju-jitsu, introduced into the Hawaiian Islands in 1941. Large following world-wide, but particularly in the United States under Ed Parker, who systemized the art to make it especially suitable for Americans.

Koei-Kan. Japanese, founded by Eizo Onishi in 1952. Includes training in both free-fighting and in forms based on the Naha-te and Shuri-te forms. Not widely known, although there are active factions in the U.S., Europe, and South America.

Kyokushinkai. Japanese, founded by Masutatsu Oyama. Considerable emphasis on sparring and board-breaking ability. Influenced heavily by both the circular Chinese styles and Japanese Shotokan karate.

Pa-Kua. Chinese, one of the three major internal systems which emphasize inner strength. The others are Hsing-I and Tai Chi Chuan.

Praying Mantis. Major Chinese style of Kung-fu, founded in the 17th century by Wang Lang in southern China. Very popular on the U.S. West Coast, as well as other areas across America.

Rembukai. Japanese style developed in the 1950s, incorporating elements of Chinese Kempo and Okinawan karate. Although popular in Japan, few schools exist in the United States.

Shito-Ryu. Japanese, one of the major styles. Founded in 1930 by Kenwa Mabuni, an Okinawan master of Shuri-te and Naha-te. Emphasizes basics, forms, and sparring, as well as forms using ancient Oriental weapons.

Shorei-Ryu. Okinawan, derivative of the old Naha-te system. Great emphasis on variety in hand techniques, and Shorei-Ryu forms (the mainstay of the style) are filled with punching, ripping, gouging, holding, and throwing techniques using the hands.

Shorin-Ryu. One of the two original karate styles of Okinawa (along with Shorei-Ryu), with roots in the old Shuri-te system. Three sub-systems of Shorin-Ryu now exist, including Shobayashi-Ryu (small forest school), Kobayashi-Ryu (young forest school), and Matsubayashi-Ryu (pine forest school). All three refer to the pine forest where the original Shaolin Temple was located in China. Shorin-Ryu is based on Shaolin, and is considered to have had the greatest influence of all the original systems on karate as we know it today.

Shotokan. Japanese, literally the "hall of Shoto." Founded when Gichin Funakoshi, a famous karate master, moved from Okinawa to Japan in the late 1920s. Shotokan is based on Okinawan Shorei-Ryu and Shorin-Ryu, and the name refers to the place in which the style was first practiced (Funakoshi's writing name was "Shoto"). Today Shotokan still remains the most widespread of the Japanese styles, and probably has the largest enrollment worldwide. Many other styles, including the enormously popular Wado-Ryu, are based on the early Shotokan teachings of Master Funakoshi.

Tai Chi Chuan. Chinese, one of the oldest systems of kung-fu. Although designed originally as a fighting art, Tai Chi is practiced today more as an exercise system. Very popular in China, being practiced daily by tens of millions of followers. Widespread throughout the world, although with fewer followers than the more flamboyant forms of martial arts.

Tae Kwon Do. Korean, literally the "art of kicking and punching." Based on the ancient Korean martial arts of Taekyon and Subak, Tae Kwon Do also incorporates some Okinawan karate forms and Chinese blocking techniques. Although Tae Kwon Do is somewhat of a catch-all name for Korean-style karate, definite sub-systems do exist, including the popular Moo Duk Kwan, Ji Do Kwan, and Chung Do Kwan. General Choi Hong Hi, a military man, is credited with organizing Tae Kwon Do as we know it today. Enormously popular in Korea, where it is part of the required curriculum for school children, and now quite widespread throughout the United States and Europe.

Tang Soo Do. A popular Korean type of karate very similar to Tae Kwon Do. Based on the old Korean art of Subak, with great Chinese influence also. Developed by Hwang Kee during the years 1936 to 1945. The most famous of Tang Soo Do practioners is Chuck Norris, a former karate Champion and now a film star.

Uechi-Ryu. Okinawan, named after the founder, Kanbum Uechi, who developed the style during the 1930s. Heavy Chinese influence dominates the style, with low kicks, short stances, and circular blocks. Okinawan Shorei-Ryu also plays heavily into the characteristics of Uechi-Ryu. Although widespread throughout Okinawa and the United States, Uechi-Ryu stresses great body conditioning, and fewer schools have emerged than with some other styles.

Wado-Ryu. Japanese, one of the original styles branching from the teachings of Gichin Funakoshi in the 1930s. Founded by Hironori Otsuka, a jutitsu master, Wado-Ryu is considered, along with Shotokan, to be one of the "classical" Japanese styles, having no Chinese, Korean, or Okinawan influence other than that included in Funakoshi's original teachings. The name means "Way of Peace (or Harmony)." Along with Shotokan, Goju-Ryu, Shito-Ryu, and Kyokushinkai, Wado-Ryu is thought to have one of the largest worldwide followings.

Washin-Ryu. Japanese, one of the lesser-known styles in the U.S. The leader of the style, Hidy Ochiai, resides in the United States, where Washin-Ryu now makes it's headquarters. The style's founder is unknown, although it's history dates back to the 16th century.

Wing Chun. Chinese, probably the best known of all Kung-fu styles. Although predominately composed of hand techniques, Wing Chun enjoys a large following in the Orient, Europe, and the Americas. The style gained publicity when Bruce Lee, the famous martial arts film star of the 1970s, announced it as a style in which he trained.

Wu Shu. Chinese, actually a name encompassing most forms of kung-fu, similar to the usage of the word "Tae Kwon Do" in Korean. The emphasis in pure Wu Shu is on forms rather than fighting, with heavy usage of the traditional Chinese Sword, knife, staff, and spear weapons.

Major Non-Karate Systems of Martial Arts

Aikido. Japanese, a defensive system of throws and holds stressing reflexes, rhythmic movement, and internal strength.

Arnis. Phillipines, a style of offensive and defensive movements mostly using weapons (mainly sticks), although some empty-handed blocks and strikes are also included.

Iaido. Japanese, the art of the drawing and cutting of the samurai sword against an opponent. Many times combined during teaching with Kendo.

Judo. Japanese, founded by Jigoro Kano in 1882, and the first martial art to be introduced to the U.S. A system using throws, joint locks, choke holds, and some strikes. Originally for self-defense, judo has now become important as a sport worldwide, including Olympic competition.

Ju-Jitsu. Japanese, a self-defense system incorporating the throws and holds of aikido and judo with some of the strikes of karate. One of the oldest of Japanese martial arts, and the source of many of the techniques we see today in judo and karate.

Kendo. Japanese, the art of swordsmanship. Very popular in Japan, with a heavy emphasis on the traditions of this old Japanese art.

Kobu-Jutsu. Okinawan, the art of the ancient weapons. Many karate styles incorporate some kobu-jutsu into their curriculum, with the primary weapons being the tonfa, the nunchaku, the bo, the sai, and the kama.

Ninjutsu. An art based on the ancient Japanese discipline of the trained assassin. Incorporates karate, kendo, kobu-jutsu, and various espionage practices.

Savate. French, a style of foot and fist fighting similar to karate. Popular in that country during the 1800s, although overtaken in popularity now by karate.

Muay Thai. Thailand, the native form of sport karate fighting. A very brutal sport, Muay Thai allows punches with gloved hands, and foot, knee, and elbow strikes using unpadded weapons. Because of the viciousness of the sport, Muay Thai has little or no support outside of Thailand, and is not practiced as a sport in the United States.

Sumo. The ancient Japanese style of wrestling. Although diminished in popularity, sumo events still draw large crowds in Japan, and are steeped in the traditions of that country.

APPENDIX C
Belt Advancement Requirements and Record

Grade Number	Color	General Requirements	Date Rec'd	Test Grade	Instructor Testing

APPENDIX D
Tournament Forms and Light Contact Fighting Rules

These rules appear courtesy Rainbow Publications and *Karate Illustrated* magazine. Copyright by Ohara Publications. These rules may not be reprinted in part or total except by special permission through *Karate Illustrated* and Ohara Publications.

FORMS COMPETITION
Contestants
All contestants must present themselves suitably attired (as described in earlier section under Contestants) and ready to compete. They should be divided into separate divisions based on style, or the origin of the form to be executed.

Suitability of Officials
An official in any way affiliated with a contestant may continue to sit as a judge, as long as the high and low scores received by a competitor are nullified in the determination of divisional winners. Seven rather than five judges are recommended for finals competition. The suitability of all officials shall be determined by the promoter, his arbitrator, or the promoter's governing regional body.

Scoring
The officials shall each award scores on the basis of 10.0 for a perfect routine, with the use of decimal intervals. The 10.0 points are awarded as follows: for *showmanship*—2.0, for *difficulty*—3.0, and for *execution*—5.0 points.

The scorekeeper shall carefully record the scores dictated to him by an assistant. After marking down scores he shall eliminate the highest and lowest marks, using the sum of the remaining evaluations for the grading of the performance. (*Note:* If the marks of the officials on one routine are 7.0, 7.0, 7.5, 6.0, 8.0, the highest mark in this hypothetical situation (8.0) and the lowest mark (6.0) are discarded.) The three intermediate marks of 7.0, 7.0 and 7.5 are added together making the valuation of the routine 21.5. In the event that there are two or more identical high marks, only one will be discarded. The same applies for the low marks. Average scores vary from region to region. As a consideration to the promoter and local competitors, judges should be willing and able to comply with standards existing in different areas. It is up to a promoter and his arbitrators to explain to judges from out of town what the scoring norms are for forms competition in the area.

Scoring Showmanships
The highest point values shall be awarded for overall martial expressiveness and beauty of composition. The ideal contestant will make a strong entrance and exit from the competition area. When performing, the intensity of his movements, the variations in his rhythm, the focus of his eyes, and the changes in his facial expressions will make his routine come to life. The officials should be able to visualize the contestant's imaginary opponent as he executes the different fighting techniques.

When a musical performance is permitted, the contestant must also be evaluated on his ability to use the music to enhance the routine. His selection of music should allow for a variety of rhythms, with slow and fast passages. Too long an introductory musical passage must be regarded as poor form and graded down.

The contestant's movements should be synchronized with the music, and his routine must terminate precisely with the music. A kata routine which is shorter or longer than the music shall be penalized.

Scoring Difficulty
Routines which demonstrate the widest range of techniques shall be given the highest point values. A routine composed entirely of hand techniques cannot be scored as highly as a routine which shows a balance between hand and foot techniques. The officials and contestants should be aware of the difference between show kata and traditional kata. Still a routine which is executed with great visible effort, or

which is hardly mastered, must be seriously downgrated. Additionally, *any form lasting longer than two minutes should be penalized by the judges and downgraded accordingly.*

Scoring Fairly

Judges are asked to remember that kata and form vary from system to system and teacher to teacher. Therefore a form should not be judged according to whether or not a competitor executes technique sequences exactly the way they were taught to the judge.

Scoring Execution

In an artistic performance, the martial artist must show that he is the master of his body and its movements, and that he can complete his routine with control, ease, style and exactitude. With this in mind, the officals must first look for good posture, continuity and proper technique.

In addition, **hard style** execution shall be evaluated on the following basis:
1. *Balance* — particularly during the transition between techniques;
2. *Stance Work* — each front stance, back stance, horse stance, and cat stance must show a consistency of height and width throughout the routine;
3. *Focused Power* — techniques must be concentrated, and visibly forceful;
4. *Purpose* — techniques must show an offensive or defensive purpose;

Soft style execution, on the other hand, shall be evaluated on a different basis:

1. *Balance* — particularly before and after an acrobatic technique;
2. *Fluidity* — the transition between techniques must be smooth, with a flowing elegance;
3. *Vigor* — techniques must contain energy and power.

Coaching

Neither instructors nor fellow students are permitted to speak, signal, nor in any way coach a contestant during his performance. Nor may they attempt in any way to influence the officials in their decisions.

Unsportsmanlike Conduct

Rude, vulgar or abusive behavior on the part of a contestant, an instructor, or a fellow student shall result in the immediate disqualification of the contestant at issue.

Ties

If the competition ends with two or more contestants holding identical scores, the tied contestants may elect to repeat the same routine they performed and tied with or choose another. If the contestants are *still* tied, they will each be required to perform a *different* routine. If they are still tied, the judges shall be required to point to the winning competitor. A majority vote shall determine the winner. High and low scores are not reinserted to break ties or determine winners.

A Competitor Who Forgets His Form

A competitor who forgets his form may so inform the judges. When they have been informed, they shall allow the competitor to start again. Each judge shall deduct one whole point from the competitor's eventual score. A competitor who forgets his form again is declared disqualified.

Order of Performance

All forms competitors are equally entitled to benefit from the luck of the draw. Hence all competitors draw numbers from a hat or other suitable container in each round of competition — eliminations, semi-finals and finals. No other method of determining the order of performance is acceptable.

Weapons

Only authentic martial arts weapons which are kept under the constant control of the contestant's limbs are suitable for competition. Throwing stars, darts, arrows, and flying projectiles of any kind may not be used (the rope dart, securely attached to a rope is an exception). Rubber nunchaku, plastic swords and other training weapons are not allowed.

The referee shall inspect all weapons prior to competition. Any weapon which the referee feels might endanger the audience or the contestant, due to worn parts or poor construction, may not be used.

Scoring the Weapons Routine

The officials must bear in mind that a weapon is an extension of the arms and legs. The contestant must show that he is the master of both body and weapon. When performing, the strength of his movements, the control over his weapon, and the ease of transition between techniques must all attest to a perfect coordination of body with weapon.

Also, the choice of weapon and routine must correspond to the capability of the competitor. A contestant who chooses a weapon too heavy to wield with control and power, or who swings the weapon around without any relationship between body movement and weapon technique, must be seriously downgraded.

Light Contact Fighting Rules

Contestants

Each contestant must present himself to the referee as suitably attired and physically prepared to compete. He or she must wear a traditional or professional karate or kung fu uniform in a good state of repair. Topless competitors or sleeveless uniforms are no longer acceptable in a sport hoping to attract a public following outside the field of martial arts. T-shirts are permitted if they are part of a school uniform and list the name of the school or style of the competitor. Jewelry or any object which the referee feels might endanger either the fighter or his opponent may not be worn. A competitor with offensive words or art work on the uniform may be denied the privilege of participation. A competitor must also have the safety equipment required in his division. As nearly as possible, contestants shall be matched according to age, sex, weight, and proficiency in fighting divisions to be determined by the promoter. For the purpose of identification, a referee may require a competitor to wear a colored flag or pennant which shall be attached to the back of his ranking belt.

Length of the Contest

A tournament match shall last a total of two minutes running time or a total of two minutes minus the time that elapses during any official time out. Only the center referee may call for a time out. A competitor who has scored the most points after two minutes shall be declared the winner of the match. Any five-point spread shall determine a winner, whether or not the two-minute time has elapsed. Thus, scores of 5-0, 6-1, 7-2, etc., are declared winning scores. An exception to this occurs in grand championship matches, which shall run for two two-minute rounds and will be scored on a total point basis.

Sudden Death

If at the end of two minutes fighting the score is tied, competitors shall be allowed 30 seconds recovery time and the match shall be resumed. Victory shall go to the first competitor to score a point.

Number of Officials

Each elimination match shall be conducted by at least one referee and two mobile judges. These shall be assisted by both a timekeeper and a scorekeeper. The suitability of all officials shall be determined by the tournament promoter. All evening finals matches shall be officiated by four corner judges, a referee, a timekeeper, and a scorekeeper. Evening finals judges shall be from different areas of the country (as far as possible).

Duties of the Timekeeper

The timekeeper shall be seated adjacent to the fighting area and shall stop and start time according to the referee's signal to do so. He shall, by an agreed-upon signal, inform the referee when time has run out. Time runs out, officially, only when the judges and fighters have been verbally informed of the fact by the center referee.

Duties of the Scorekeeper

The scorekeeper shall keep count of all scores awarded to competitors by the center referee.

Calling Time Out

Only the referee may call a time out. He may do so for any of the following reasons: 1) to allow equipment adjustment; 2) to administer voting among the officials 3) to award points, assess penalties, administer warnings; 4) to return contestants to the center, neutral area of the ring; 5) to attend an injured contestant; 6) to hear a legal protest.

A competitor may never call his own time out, though a reasonable, timely request for a brief time out ought not to be denied.

Duties of the Judges

The judges shall be black belts. At an A-rated tournament they should be black belts with recent judging experience. They are required to limit their motions to their respective areas of the ring. Their motions should not bring them in bounds and they should make efforts never to interfere with the motions of the referee or fighters.

Voting for Points

When the referee believes there has been a significant exchange of technique, or when signaled to do so by the voice of a corner judge, he shall call out the word "stop!" in a loud voice. He shall then return the competitors to the center of the ring and address the judges by saying, "Judges, call!"

Recommended Safety Equipment

For tournaments held on concrete floors, head protection is strongly suggested to protect the front and back of the head from dangerous and potentially fatal falls. Shin and forearm guards, and breast protectors for women are highly recommended. Most of the country's top competitors will not compete without the mandatory and recommended equipment.

Calls a Judge May Make

The referee calls a halt to the fighting with the word, "Stop!" He returns the fighters to the center of the ring and says, "Judges, call!" He casts his vote simultaneously with the other judges.

1. *Point* — If flags are used, a judge raises an appropriate flag (red or white) to indicate his opinion about which finger at the competitor who has scored.
2. *No Point* — A judge crosses his flags or forearms at waist level to indicate that no point was scored.
3. *Penalty* — A judge holds both flags or arms in such a way as to point at the feet of the offending competitor. This means he thinks something that happened in the match calls for a penalty.
4. *Point and Penalty* — May not be awarded to the same competitor. One competitor may be awarded a point while the other is penalized. The judge signals for this by holding the arm or the flag of the scoring competitor out and pointing the other flag or arm at the feet of the offending competitor.
5. *Clash* — With or without flags a judge makes a motion as though he were hitting both fists or the tips of both flags together. This means that the judge believes points were scored simultaneously. Hence, the judge believes no point should be awarded.
6. *Out* — A corner judge calls the word, "Out!" when in his opinion a player has stepped out of bounds until the referee calls the word, "Stop!" which halts the action. A judge indicates that in his opinion a player was out of bounds by pointing the appropriate flag or arm at the area where the offending competitor stepped out.

What a Point Is

A point is a legal, legitimate and controlled martial arts technique scored by a player in bounds that strikes an opponent with light to moderate force to a legal target area. A point is legitimate if as a martial arts technique it held in reserve the capacity to physically injure or momentarily stun an opponent. A point is controlled if it appears to strike an opponent with a great deal less than its potential force, and if it was executed by a competitor who was not falling down or running away at the time, and who did not fall down because of improper or unbalanced execution of the technique after it struck the opponent.

How a Point is Awarded

Points are awarded by a majority vote of all ring judges. The majority of the judges do not have to consult or agree on the techniques being scored (and should not consult on the matter).

Legal Target Areas — Head and face, side of neck (but not throat), ribs, chest, abdomen, collarbone, groin, and kidneys. *Note: The Groin* — Becomes a legal or an illegal technique at the discretion of the tournament promoter. Competitors are advised to inquire about the legality of groin techniques before fighting.

Legal Techniques — All controlled martial arts techniques delivered to legal targets with legal surfaces except those listed following as illegal.

Illegal Target Areas — Spine, back of neck, throat, hip, elbow, knee, buttocks, entire leg, and feet (except when sweeps are allowed).

Illegal Techniques — Head butts, hair pulls, bites, scratching techniques thrown with elbows and knees, over-the-shoulder throws, any sweeps higher than mid-calf level, stomps to the head of any kind, any jump on a downed opponent, kicks to the legs, deliberate and repeated kicks to the hip, *any blind technique of questionable control considered dangerous to an opponent by a voting majority of the judges and center referee.*

Non-target Areas—Arms, shoulder, and hands. Repeated attacks to these areas will result in penalization.

Sweeps and Takedowns, Grabs and Ground Techniques — Sweeps and takedowns are allowed only on wooden, carpeted, or otherwise padded floors, never on concrete, tile or terrazo. When legal, the sweep or takedown itself is but a means to an end — scoring. A point is only given when the takedown is effectively and legally followed up. Judo throws, over-the-shoulder reaps or hip throws are not allowed. Sweeps must be executed at mid-calf or below and must be executed to the back of the legs in an attempt to topple the opponent backwards. If a sweep is recklessly executed or no attempt is made to score when the opponent has been downed, the sweep will be judged illegal and the fighter penalized one point. A repeat of the same situation during the bout or any subsequent bout will result in disqualification for the offending competitor. Only a hand technique (to any legal target) or a carefully controlled kick or stomp to the body will be allowed on a downed opponent (one foot must be on the ground throughout the stomp or kick). Never under any circumstances may a player stomp to his opponent's head. A competitor may grab the gi of his opponent in an attempt to score. He shall be allowed to grip the gi for one second, after which time if there has been no score the gi must be released. Likewise the gi pants may be grabbed. A kick may be trapped or grabbed, but only for purposes of executing a counterattack to an upright opponent. Sweeping or reaping an opponent with his kicking leg elevated is dangerous and therefore illegal.

Scoring on the Ground

Once a player is on the floor, his opponent will have two seconds to score on him, after which time the referee shall call time. A player who deliberately drops the ground shall have the same two-second period in which to score (a drop kick only). A player who is on the ground because of an illegal takedown or sweep may not be scored on. If both players end up on the ground following a sweep attempt, either may attempt to score within the allotted two seconds.

Contact

Light Contact — all contact is made with safety equipment only. Light contact means there is no penetration or visible movement of the opponent as a result of the

technique. Head face, side of neck, collarbone, kidneys, spine, and groin, can only be attacked with light contact. In addition, it should be noted that light contact must be made to these areas in brown and black belt divisions for a point to be scored.
Moderate Contact—slight penetration or slight target movement. Moderate contact may be made to the chest, ribcage, and abdomen. Light contact must be made to these areas in order for the technique to be considered a point.
Excessive Contact — a call for excessive contact indicates that the judge or referee saw a competitor strike his opponent with force in excess of the force necessary to have scored a point. Though it is largely a judgment call, indicates that contact has been excessive are to be seen in the following reactions:
1. Visible snapping back of a competitor's head from the force of a blow.
2. A knockdown of an opponent (not recklessly charging into a technique or occurring in instances where the fallen party neither fell nor slipped).
3. A knockout of an opponent.
4. The appearance of severe swelling or bleeding. (Bleeding or other obvious external injury is of itself grounds for contact even if the judges didn't see the technique).
5. The violent distortion of the body from the force of a blow to the body.

How Excessive Contact is Voted On

If a majority of all judges agree that a player is guilty of excessive contact, or, if the referee believes that a player has been guilty of excessive contact that has gone unseen by other judges, the offending player may be penalized one point. *Disqualification on an excessive contact call requires a majority of judges.* The referee may overrule corner judges who are calling for a point in order to penalize a player for excessive contact. A referee, however, may not overrule a majority of judges who vote to penalize a player for contact in order to call a point.

Other Causes of Penalization

1. Attacking illegal targets.
2. Using illegal techniques (including illegal sweeps).
3. Running out of the ring to avoid fighting (fighting out does not apply).
4. Falling to the floor to avoid attack (a player attempting a drop kick is exempt from penalty. Though if he attacks illegal targets in attempting to defend himself he should be penalized).
5. Continuing after being ordered to stop (second punching).
6. Pushing, cursing, or vindictive conduct.
7. Gross disrespect to judges or opponents (a player's friends, coach or fellow students may cause penalty under this rule).
8. Continuing negligent or reckless attacks (whether or not actual contact is ever made).

Method of Penalization

Powers of the Referee — The referee is expected to be the most experienced of the judges. He shall be empowered to issue warnings and penalty points on his own judgement, even when his viewpoint is not shared by the remaining judges. In fact, he may overrule a point vote by judges in order to assess a penalty point, since a player may not receive a penalty and a point on the same call. A referee may call for a vote by the corner judges with respect to issuing a penalty point if he is not sure that an infraction has taken place. A referee may not, however, overrule a majority of judges in order to award a point when they have voted for a penalty.

Severity of the First Offense

The severity of the first offense shall be the deciding factor in instances where the referee must decide between a warning and a penalty point. If they are serious infractions, a referee may issue a penalty point for all first offenses except for running out of the ring or falling down to avoid being scored on. A competitor must be warned at least once before he can be penalized for these two infractions. (The referee should be specific in his warning, and within hearing of the judges and his opponent. For example, "The next time you run out of the ring, you're going to lose a point. Understand?" He should wait for the competitor to acknowledge his official warning before allowing the fight to continue.)

Second Offense (Same Infraction)

On the second offense for the same rule infraction, a penalty point must be awarded to the competitor's opponent. A penalty point may be assessed for any second offense, whether or not for the same infraction, if the second infraction is deemed a major one by the center referee. Any second offense which is serious in nature may be grounds for disqualification. The referee may stop the action, assemble the judges, and with a majority vote, disqualify the offender.

Third Offense

A third offense for any combination of rule infractions requires that the player be given a penalty point. If the offense is serious, the referee may administer a disqualification vote as stated.

Injured Player

If, in the opinion of the referee or medical personnel, a player is unable to continue because of injury caused by his opponent, the offending player shall be automatically disqualified.

Unsportsmanlike Conduct

Rude, vulgar or abusive behavior on the part of a contestant, instructor, or other spectator shall result in the immediate disqualification of the contestant at issue. Such a decision is to be made by a majority of judges or the tournament arbitrator or promoter.

Running Out of Bounds to Avoid Being Scored On, or Falling Down to Avoid Being Scored On

A player who runs out of bounds to avoid being scored on or falls down to avoid being scored on will be warned on his first offense, and penalized on his second and all subsequent offenses.

Out-of-Bounds

For the purpose of scoring on his opponent, a player is out of bounds as soon as one foot touches down outside the ring boundary. However, action will continue until the referee gives the stop command.

An out-of-bounds player may be scored on by his opponent so long as his opponent has both feet in the ring when he scores with a hand technique, or the supporting leg in bounds when he scores with a kick. In the event of a jumping technique, the player must land with the non-kicking foot in bounds in order to score. A player who is out-of-bounds may be scored on and must defend himself until the referee calls a halt to the exchange. *It should be noted that it is the referee's voice, rather than the stepping out or the judge's voice, which signals an end of scoring opportunities for the aggressive opponent.*

APPENDIX E
PKA World Full-Contact Karate Champions — Past and Present

ATOMWEIGHT (under 113 lbs.)
(established 1981)

Title vacant
(established 1981)

FLYWEIGHT (113-118.9 lbs.)
(established 1981)

Jerry "The Sting" Clarke (Bradenton, Florida)
(1983 - present)

BANTAMWEIGHT (119-125.9 lbs.)
(established 1979)

Vernon "Thunderkick" Mason
(Richmond, Virginia) (1979-1980)

Larry Sanders
(Indianapolis, Indiana)   (1980)

Felipe Garcia (Denver, Colorado)
(1980-1984)

Edmund Ardissone (Nice, France)
(February-September 1984)

Felipe Garcia (Denver, Colorado)
(September 1984 - present)

FEATHERWEIGHT (126-132.9 lbs.)
(established 1975, formerly known as Superlightweight)

Gordon Franks (Minneapolis, Minnesota)
(1975-1980)

Cliff "Magic" Thomas (El Paso, Texas)
(1980-1981)

Paul Vizzio (New York, New York)
(1981 - present)

LIGHTWEIGHT (133-139.9 lbs.)
(established 1974)

Isaias Duenas (Mexico City, Mexico)
(1974-1976)

Benny "The Jet" Urquidez
(Tarzana, California)   (1976-1977)

Tommy Williams (Oklahoma City) (1981-1982)

Cliff "Magic" Thomas (El Paso, Texas)
(1982-1983)

Tony "Tiger" Rosser (Memphis, Tennessee)
(1983)

Cliff "Magic" Thomas (El Paso, Texas)
(1983 - present)

LIGHTWELTERWEIGHT (140-147.9 lbs.)
(established 1982, formerly known as Superwelterweight)

Tommy Williams
(Oklahoma City, Oklahoma)
(1982-1984)
title vacated 1984

WELTERWEIGHT (148-155.9 lbs.)
(established 1975)

Eddie Andujar (Vineland, New Jersey)
(1975-1976)

Earnest Hart, Jr. (St. Louis, Missouri)
(1976-1977)

Bobby Ryan (Providence, Rhode Island)
(1978)

Steve Shepherd (West Palm Beach, Florida)
(1978)

Earnest Hart, Jr. (St. Louis, Missouri)
(1978-1979)

Steve Shepherd (West Palm Beach, Florida)
(1979-1980)

Earnest Hart, Jr. (St. Louis, Missouri)
(1980-1981)

Jeff Gripper (Atlanta, Georgia)
(1981-1982)

Alvin Prouder (Los Angeles, California)
(1982 - present)

LIGHTMIDDLEWEIGHT (156-163.9 lbs.) Bob "Thunder" Thurman
(established 1982, formerly known as (Kansas City, Kansas)
Supermiddleweight (1982 - present)

MIDDLEWEIGHT (164-171.9 lbs.) Bill "Superfoot" Wallace
(Los Angeles, California)
(1974-1980)

Jean-Yves Theriault (Ottawa, Ontario, Canada)
(1980 - present)

LIGHTHEAVYWEIGHT (172-179.9 lbs.) Jeff Smith (Washington, D.C.)
(established 1974) (1974-1980)

Dan Macaruso (Providence, Rhode Island)
(1980-1982)

Kerry "Superkicks" Roop (Detroit, Michigan)
(1982)

Emilio Narvaez (Vineland, New Jersey)
(1983-1984)

Dennis Alexio (Davis, California)
(September 1984 - present)

HEAVYWEIGHT (180-194.9 lbs.) Joe Lewis (Los Angeles, California)
(1974-1975)

Teddy Limoz (Honolulu, Hawaii)   (1976)

Ross Scott (Indianapolis, Indiana)
(1977-1980)

Demetrius "Oaktree" Edwards
(Greenville, North Carolina)   (1980-1982)

Anthony "Amp" Elmore
(Memphis, Tennessee)   (1982)

Brad Hefton (Rockford, Illinois)
(1983 - present)

SUPERHEAVYWEIGHT (195 lbs. & over) Anthony "Amp" Elmore
(established 1982) (Memphis, Tennessee)   (1982-present)

APPENDIX F
Personal Advancement Record

Week	Techniques Learned	Forms Learned	Instructor
1.			
2.			
3.			
4.			
5.			
6.			
7.			
8.			
9.			
10.			
11.			
12.			
13.			
14.			
15.			
16.			
17.			
18.			
19.			
20.			
21.			
22.			

MUSCLES OF THE BODY

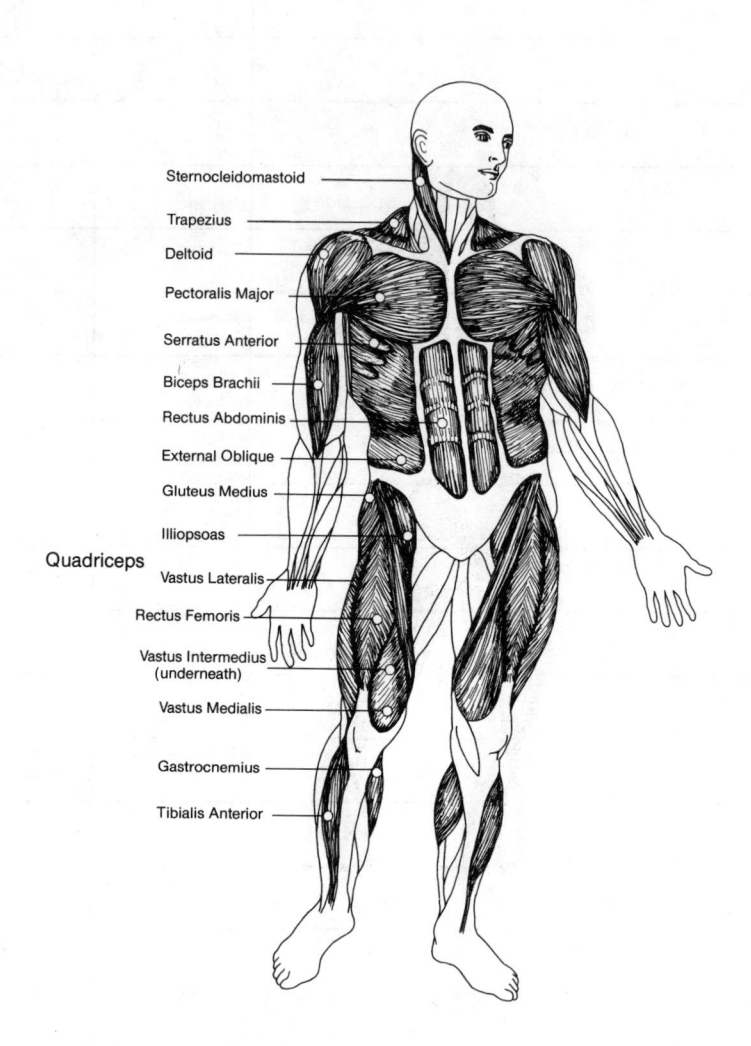

- Sternocleidomastoid
- Trapezius
- Deltoid
- Pectoralis Major
- Serratus Anterior
- Biceps Brachii
- Rectus Abdominis
- External Oblique
- Gluteus Medius
- Illiopsoas
- Quadriceps
  - Vastus Lateralis
  - Rectus Femoris
  - Vastus Intermedius (underneath)
  - Vastus Medialis
- Gastrocnemius
- Tibialis Anterior

MUSCLES OF THE BODY

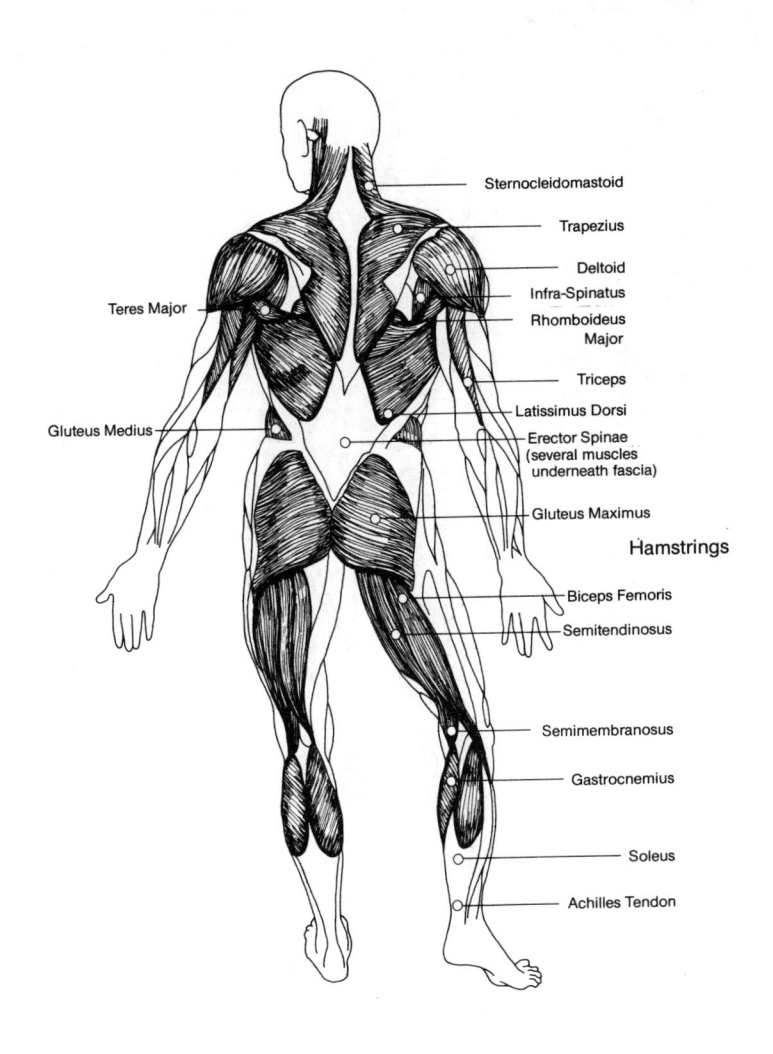

- Sternocleidomastoid
- Trapezius
- Deltoid
- Infra-Spinatus
- Rhomboideus Major
- Teres Major
- Triceps
- Latissimus Dorsi
- Gluteus Medius
- Erector Spinae (several muscles underneath fascia)
- Gluteus Maximus
- Hamstrings
- Biceps Femoris
- Semitendinosus
- Semimembranosus
- Gastrocnemius
- Soleus
- Achilles Tendon